Praise for *From Tabloid to Truth*

I have followed Dan Wooding's extraordinary career now for nearly a quarter of a century and we have worked closely with him on mission's trips to places like Poland, Uganda, Israel and Northern Ireland. His dedication to getting out the story of the Persecuted Church is close to my heart and in this powerful book you will read how he went from working for Billy Graham's London newspaper, to a period in the British tabloids and then how God turned his life around in a powerful way so he can now be a "voice" for the voiceless.

Mike MacIntosh
Pastor of Horizon Christian Fellowship, San Diego, California, and founder of Horizon International Ministries.

Dan Wooding is one of the most articulate journalists writing today. Calling attention to the plight of the persecuted people of faith, his powerful and heartfelt words sensitize Americans afresh to the value of religious freedom and the horrors of intolerance. His journey from tabloid to truth promises to be a great read.

Dean Jones
Actor

Also by Dan Wooding

Junkies are People Too
Stresspoint
I Thought Terry Dene Was Dead
Exit The Devil (with Trevor Dearing)
Train of Terror (with Mini Loman)
Rick Wakeman, the Caped Crusader
King Squealer (with Maurice O'Mahoney)
Farewell Leicester Square (with Henry Hollis)
Uganda Holocaust (with Ray Barnett)
Miracles in Sin City (with Howard Cooper)
God's Smuggler to China (with Brother David and
Sarah Bruce)
Prophets of Revolution (with Peter Asael Gonzales)
Brother Andrew
Guerilla for Christ (with Salu Daka Ndebele)
Million Dollar Promise (with Duane Logsdon)
Twenty-Six Lead Soldiers
Secret Missions
Singing In The Dark (with Barry Taylor)
Lost for Words (with Stuart Mill)
Let There Be Light (with Roger Oakland)
Rock Priest (with David Pierce)
He Intends Victory
Only Believe (with Hannu Haukka)
A Light To India (with Lillian Doerksen)
Blind Faith (with Anne Wooding)
Never Say Never

From Tabloid to Truth

The inspiring autobiography of
Christian journalist Dan Wooding
and his worldwide search for truth

Dan Wooding

Theatron Books

Enjoy bonus stories and photos at
www.FromTabloidToTruth.com

Published by Theatron Books
An imprint of Theatron Media Group
Post Office Box 606
Hemet, CA 92546-0606
Visit us at: www.TheatronBooks.com

ISBN: 0-9747163-5-9

Publisher's Cataloging-in-Publication Data

Wooding, Dan.
   From tabloid to truth : the inspiring autobiography of Christian journalist Dan Wooding and his worldwide search for truth / Dan Wooding.— [1st ed.].
    p. cm.
   ISBN: 0-9747163-5-9
1. Wooding, Dan. 2. Christian biography. 3. Journalists— Biography. 4. Journalists—Great Britain—Biography. 5. Children of missionaries—Biography. 6. Journalism, Religious. 7. Missions, British. I. Title.

BR1725.W66 F76 2004
270.8'2'092 B—-dc21

Printed in the United States of America

*Dedicated to my wife Norma
and to the memory of my parents,
Alf and Anne Wooding*

Contents

Foreword

I have known Dan Wooding for many years and this book tells us much about God's dealings in his life-sometimes with charming simplicity.

Amazing how many people he knows. One day he drove me through London and, passing under a railway bridge, he pointed to a flower-seller [Buster Edwards] and said casually: "One of the men from the 'Great Train Robbery.'"

But all that is not so important; of far more value is that he now knows and meets God's children in the suffering church. And that, I truly believe, is how God looks at our lives; how much do we do to get in touch with our brothers and sisters behind the "curtains?" How much do our lives count for that "suffering body of Christ?" I must ask myself that question, too, continuously.

To me the value of this book is to show how God guides a young man and trains him in secular work, to make his life count where it is so much needed: for the suffering church.

I therefore strongly recommend this book to a wide public, and my prayer is that you will be turned on to the most important battle that takes place in the world today: the battle for the minds of people, where the soldiers are of lead; twenty-six of them might win that war.

Brother Andrew
Harderwijk, Holland

Introduction

In the 35 years I have known Dan Wooding, there has never been one second of any day where Dan has not made full use of the talents that God gave him, although he has had his moments, especially during his "exploratory journalistic days" that perhaps may even have surprised God a little!

Dan's journey through life has been remarkable to witness. He has, I think, seen everything, (and I really mean that) and can count amongst his friends, ex-prostitutes, former drug addicts, AIDS victims, past pornographers and even members of the clergy!

Dan is a "doer." He is a rare breed. A huge percentage of the human race are either "thinkers" and never realize God's Will given to each and every one of us, or they take more than they ever give back. Dan has given his life to others and that is something very special. I always said that Dan should never have written this book as he really can't see himself as others do and therefore is not truly qualified to tell his life story as it really is, but as I have already said... Dan is a "doer"... and so he's done it!

It's hard to sum up Dan in a few paragraphs but I have done the best I can. On a car journey from Los Angeles airport to Orange County, I once asked Mr. Wooding to name me one person he knew who had led a normal life.

He failed.

In fact we could have driven to Mexico City and he still couldn't have given me an answer.

That's just one example of why I love the man with all my heart and I know God does too. I was once asked what my definition of a Christian was and without thinking, answered... Dan Wooding. Says it all really.

Rick Wakeman
Rock Musician
London, England

1
A Trip Into Terror And Love

Tuesday, September 11, 2001, seemed like just another day for my traveling companions and me as we enjoyed our tour of the Holy Land, sponsored by the Jordanian Tourist Board. They were anxious to show that Jordan was a peaceful alternative to trouble-torn Israel that was being ripped apart with violence.

The chatter on board the tourist bus was light and happy as we viewed the Jordanian countryside through the windows as it sped along the highway from Amman towards Gerasa (modern Jerash), the most complete and best-preserved Greco-Roman city in the Middle East. When we finally arrived at our destination we all climbed out and shielded our eyes to the fierce sun that was beating down on us.

Our tour guide got our group of 28 American Christian leaders and journalists organized for a photo. After the picture had been taken, we filed into the heart of the ruins of this once great city. As we walked, I talked with Giles Hudson, one of our hosts from A. Larry Ross's Dallas-based PR agency, who was waiting for a call on his mobile phone from the USA Radio Network to give a trip report. As our Jordanian guide explained about the site, Giles' mobile phone shrilled, and the guide stopped speaking for a moment.

Standing next to Giles, I waited to hear what he was going to say, but he was silent. He seemed to turn pale as he listened to the caller.

He took a deep breath and said, "A plane has just slammed into one of the Twin Towers of the World Trade Center building in New York City."

The news spread quickly to the entire team. In the buzz, many of us said that probably it was a small plane that had lost control and crashed into the huge tower. Still, it was terrible news.

In a state of shock, we slowly walked in the searing heat to the nearby city of Gadara (modern Um Qais), with its spectacular panoramic views overlooking the Sea of Galilee. This was the site where Jesus sent demented spirits out of two men into a herd of swine who ran down the hill and drowned in the Sea of Galilee (Matthew 8:28-34). There Giles received another call in which he was informed that a second plane had crashed into another of the towers.

Soon, we heard that a third plane had crashed into the Pentagon in Washington, D.C., and we realized this chain of events was not accidental. A torrent of terror had been unleashed on America which we later learned was done by a group of terrorists led by men like the suicide pilots Mohamed Atta and Marwan Al-Shehhi, who had rammed the two airliners into the World Trade Center Towers. A fourth hijacked plane crashes into a field in Somerset County, Pennsylvania, southeast of Pittsburgh.

Trading on Wall Street was immediately stopped and the Federal Aviation Administration halted all flight operations at the nation's airports for the first time in U.S. history. The U.S. military was placed on high alert.

As we waited helplessly for more information, President Bush addressed the nation and vowed to "find those responsible and bring them to justice." Hundreds of New York City firefighters and police sent to rescue WTC workers were lost when the WTC Twin Towers collapsed. Secretary of State Colin Powell identified Osama Bin Laden as the mastermind behind the devastation.

It was surreal to be in Jordan at the time of the worst terrorist attack in modern history. It was if the demons of hate had been unleashed on America and all we could do was to pray for the victims and their relatives.

As our stunned group stood discussing the situation, it hit us that we were in an Arab country and could be targets for terrorists.

We were taken by our guide to a hotel on the shores of the Dead Sea. We could hear the sounds of a violent gun-battle taking place in Jericho, just a short way across the water, that went on for most of the night. Some of the team stayed up to pray for peace not only in the Middle East, but also in America.

I spent a sleepless night in my room and eventually was able to call my wife Norma back in Southern California to assure her that we were all doing fine. Like all our loved ones back in the United States, she was concerned for our safety.

"Don't worry love," I assured her. "We are in God's hands!"

The idea for the trip began at the National Religious Broadcasters

(NRB) Convention in Dallas earlier in the year, when the Jordanian Tourist Board and the Jordan Ministry of Tourism launched an effort to educate Americans about the less explored parts of the Holy Land that extends beyond Israel. This area includes modern-day Jordan, now guardian of more than 200 major biblical sites from both Old and New Testaments.

His Majesty King Abdullah II had shared with a small group of pastors in Washington, D.C. about the history, beauty and safety of his country, and invited them to come and visit. The trip that was led by Larry Ross, who has been Billy Graham's press representative for many years, and sponsored by the Jordanian Tourist Board.

Located on the eastern side of the Jordan River, this country is blessed with the rich spiritual heritage that encompasses the full history of salvation as recorded in the Bible. Abraham, Job, Moses, Ruth, Elijah, John the Baptist and Jesus were some of the figures of the Bible who performed pivotal elements of their divinely-ordained missions in this ancient landscape that is now within the Hashemite Kingdom of Jordan.

The very name of the country—Jordan—retains the unique baptismal aura of a holy river and a blessed land. It was here, in the waters of Bethany-beyond-the-Jordan, where the Trinity of Father, Son and Holy Spirit was first manifested explicitly when John baptized Jesus.

The southern Jordan River Valley, the Dead Sea plains, and the surrounding hills and mountains are the home to some of the most momentous events in the history of man's relationship with God. Here Abraham arrived in the Holy Land; Jacob and Esau made their pact; God protected Lot while destroying Sodom and Gomorrah; Moses saw the Promised Land which he would never enter; Joshua crossed the Jordan River into Canaan; Elijah rode a "chariot of fire" into heaven; Elisha cured the leper in the waters of the river; John the Baptist preached, baptized Jesus and was killed by King Herod; and Jesus received the Holy Spirit and resisted the temptations of Satan.

God repeatedly designated Jordan as a land of peace and refuge, where Ruth, Elijah, David, Jesus, John the Baptist and the first Christian communities, among others, found safety and peace. Most of the great biblical prophets made their journeys of faith from the east bank of the Jordan River to the west, symbolically moving from the "wilderness" where men and women are tested, to the "Promised Land" that is the Kingdom of God.

We visited many of the sites precious to Christians and paused at the ancient fortress-city of Petra, which means "stone" in Greek. It was the capital of the Nabateans, who carved a wonderland of temples, tombs and elaborate buildings out of solid rock. These people had grown rich by levying taxes on travelers to ensure safe passage through their lands.

The news about the terrorism traveled fast. Even at Petra, camel drivers and donkey owners offered their condolences to us for the violence that had taken place in New York City and Washington, D.C.

As we tried to keep up with the news from the States—it was all bad—our team tried to keep a semblance of normalcy. We visited the Bethany-beyond-the-Jordan baptism site. The winding loop in the Jordan River opposite Jericho has long been considered the spot of Jesus' baptism. Here the Spirit of God descended like a dove upon Jesus, and a voice from heaven said, "This is my Son, whom I love; with him I am well pleased." (Matthew 3:17). As some of the group went down to the site, they were confronted with Jordanian and Israeli soldiers facing each other with their weapons.

It was a very unreal week. Here we were in the land of the Prince of Peace, yet there was evidence of war all around. We were in the Holy Land on a mission of good-will, all the while knowing that America had just been devastated as a result of ancient antagonisms that emanated from this region thousands of years before.

Because all flights into the United States were halted, it seemed like we would have to remain in Jordan for some time. But suddenly the good news came that Royal Jordanian Airlines had been able to negotiate a flight to JFK Airport in New York, the first Arab airline allowed back in the U.S. after the 9/11 attack.

"Before we go on to the airport, we have been invited to participate in a candlelight gathering in Amman," said Larry Ross.

Before we left for the service that would be attended by nearly 500 Jordanian Christians and Muslims, a bellboy at our hotel in Amman asked if he could address us over the bus PA system. He told us that he had lost some of his family in the fighting in the West Bank and said that he knew what it was to lose members of his family that he loved. "I would like to tell you that I am very sorry for what has happened in America and I want you to know that all of the Jordanian people share in your sorrow."

At the service we joined with others in lighting candles for peace at the Citadel in Amman. Everyone wanted to show their solidarity with the World Trade Center and Pentagon victims and their families.

Muslim clerics united with Christian priests and ministers from the various Christian communities in Jordan, as well as the Lord Mayor of Amman to condemn the violence in the United States and they prayed for the families of the victims. It was hard for us to hold back the tears at this momentous time in world history.

Father Nabil Haddad was one of those who led prayers. He was from the Melkite Catholic Church in Amman. He asked God to help join the people of the United States with the people of Jordan in this special prayer service. He said, "Heavenly father, you alone have the power to bring good out of evil. We ask you to guide the hands of all leaders and decision makers who are responding to this crisis at this very moment."

Also participating was Sheik Imad Chaehiv from the Islamic Education Center in Amman, who said that he had lived in the United States for 15 years.

In an interview, he told me, "I can't tell you how depressed I have been since this happened. I was so upset and sad. I have my family here with me and my wife was crying the whole day. I really can't express how sorry I feel for this. We condemn these actions. This is not the real Muslims that are doing something like this. This is not what the picture of the Muslims should be."

When asked what he thought about the Taliban in Afghanistan, he said, "We do not support the Taliban at all. We do not feel their word is the word of all Muslims. Most Muslims are against terrorism and against fundamentalism. Hopefully, Americans will realize this."

Standing with the Muslim sheik was Rev. Samuel Abu-Aber, a pastor at the Assemblies of God church in Amman. He said, "Our message today to the whole world is a message of love. We felt so much sorrow for what happened in the United States. We saw how many people were weeping and we felt the sorrow of the loved ones. We are united with them in their sorrow and we pray that

God can bring to them peace and that people in the future will realize that we are all from the same roots. We are all the descendents of Abraham and our message is that of love and peace."

I then spoke with Nidal Barjas Alhadid, the Lord Mayor of Amman, who said, "We share with you the feelings of anger, grief and sadness, for all that happened in the cities of New York and Washington. The attacks on innocent souls made all of us very sad. This is the kind of act that cannot be done by any human being. There must be some steps taken to control such acts and such terrorist organizations. I'd like to send my condolences to the families of the victims and pray that their souls will rest in peace."

After the service, our team headed for Amman Airport to fly back to New York. Security was tight and we understood that several armed marshals were on the flight with us.

When we arrived at JFK Airport, a bevy of armed FBI agents and other security officers met us. Like many others, I couldn't catch the flight I was booked on, so had to find another airline to get back to Southern California. As we took off, I could see the pall of smoke rising from what was the Twin Towers of the World Trade Center.

I will never forget what has happened to our world over those days. But it was heartening to know that so many from around the world were standing with the American people in love and solidarity, like our friends in Jordan.

After getting such a wonderful insight into the biblical sites of Jordan myself, I can only recommend the experience to others. It is the trip of a lifetime for biblical scholars, and a life-changing inspirational journey for those who wish to retrace the footsteps of the heroes of our faith. For our team it was a trip into terror, but also one where we experienced the love and concern of the Jordanian people. Nevertheless, all of us knew that we were now living in a world that was totally different from the one we woke up to on September 11.

The events that unfolded in New York City were unlike anything else in my years as a journalist, and I had seen plenty. I had traveled to the heart of Russia with my friend Ray Barnett, the founder of Friends in the West, during the dark days of communism that resulted in us, along with other Christians, being held under house arrest just outside of Moscow.

Over the years God gave me the opportunity to interview Mother Teresa in Calcutta, India, when she was still relatively unknown. At another point I was arrested at Lagos Airport in Nigeria on a return visit the country of my birth, and was held in a cell overnight before being deported at gunpoint.

I went to Uganda just days after Idi Amin, whose regime had murdered 500,000 Ugandans, had been driven out of the country, to write a book on the courageous survivors of the "Uganda Holocaust."

I reported on a team from Open Doors smuggling Bibles into Cuba and later survived a car bomb, placed by a terrorist group, in El Salvador. I reported on "Project Pearl" in June 1981, when one million Bibles were delivered by sea to Swatow Beach, South China by a former U.S. Marine, Brother David, whose real name was Doug Sutphen.

The Lord allowed me to be one of the first Christian journalists granted permission to visit North Korea to report direct from Pyongyang for a U.S.-based radio network. Later, I worked with Billy Graham on his historic Moscow crusade in 1991 and met Russian dissident Alexander Ogorodnikov who had spent seven years in the Gulag for his faith.

My journalistic ministry has taken me to the Middle East many times. One time I interviewed a Hamas leader in Gaza with Brother Andrew. Later, along with my wife Norma, I survived a brush with death from Islamic Jihad gunmen in Bethlehem.

AIDS has been a concern to me since the inception of the disease, and I have attended World AIDS Conferences in Japan, Canada and Spain, meeting many Christians who are involved in the HIV/AIDS battle.

During those years, I had the privilege of filing stories from countries such as Albania, Bangladesh, Burma, China, Cuba, Egypt, El Salvador, Ethiopia, Grenada, India, Jordan, Israel (including the West Bank and Gaza), Lebanon, Nicaragua, North Korea, Romania, Uganda and Vietnam.

I have also been able to interview or meet several heads of state including Richard Nixon, George and Barbara Bush, the Prime Minister of Bangladesh and the President of Uganda, to name a few.

The Christian leaders I have interviewed have included Billy

From Tabloid To Truth

Graham, Franklin Graham, Mother Teresa, Luis Palau, Coretta Scott King, Bill Bright, Pat Robertson and Charles Colson and many others. I interviewed celebrities like Robert Duvall, Pat Boone, Jane Russell, Frankie Laine, Johnny Mathis, Burt Lancaster, David Soul, Johnny Cash and many more.

Through the ups and the downs of my journalistic career, which now spans more than 35 years, the love of Jesus Christ, and that of my wife Norma, have been the two solid rocks that have kept me going.

But all of us knew that we were now living in a world that was totally different to the one we woke up to on September 11. And to think that my grand adventure of covering the news began in a small African village in 1940.

2
African Odyssey

T he shrilling of crickets, the eerie whistling of night birds and the distant howling of hyenas intruded into the still night air of the delivery ward of Vom Christian Hospital in Nigeria. It was just six days before Christmas, 1940. But there was little goodwill in a world convulsed in the mayhem of World War Two that had begun on Sunday, September 3, 1939, when Prime Minister Neville Chamberlain announced that the British Empire was at war with Germany.

As the former Austrian house painter, Adolf Schicklgruber, better known as Adolf Hitler, was trying to take over the world, I was struggling to get into it. After eight hours, I finally appeared, bawling and spluttering.

"You've got a boy, Anne," said Dr. Percy Barnden, a British missionary doctor, as he snipped my umbilical cord and then slapped a mosquito that was probing his arm. My mother smiled gently as she looked down at her first child.

My father, Alf, was anxiously waiting in our mud-walled home in Izom, a remote bush village some 600 miles away, for news of the birth. A telephone call from the hospital, operated by the Sudan United Mission, to the British government outpost in Abuja, announced my birth. Then an African messenger walked thirty miles to Izom to see my father to tell him the good news. He arrived on Friday, December 20.

"You have a son," beamed the exhausted courier to a background of bleating goats, barking dogs and shouting boys.

A cheer broke out among the many natives, that crowded into the small Wooding compound. They laughed, danced and clapped their hands. My father smiled, pride showing in his eyes. Now, he knew, would come the traditional naming ritual.

"We must call him "Dan Juma," which means "Son of Friday," said one of the natives, dressed only in a loincloth.

"Yes," the others chorused. "He is to be Dan Juma."

Much tongue clacking greeted the new name. The "resolution"

had been unanimously carried, and so my father decided not to tell them that I had, in fact, been born not on Friday, but Thursday. Talking drums quickly spread the news that "Dan Juma" had arrived.

My father packed a few belongings for the long trip to Vom, which included a twenty-four-hour truck journey to Minna and then a long rail journey to Vom, situated on the Jos Plateau. It was Christmas Eve when we met for the first time. I was a little mite, gurgling with joy, as I looked into the weather-beaten open face of a courageous little man from Liverpool who had obeyed God's call to bring the gospel to a sweltering land where millions had still not heard of Jesus Christ. Tribe after tribe had been caught in the bonds of animism, witchcraft and ancestral worship, and millions had already turned to Islam.

After a few weeks of rest for my mother, who was also from Liverpool, the three of us returned to the dusty village of Izom, a cluster of mud huts crowned with grass roofs. Many Muslims lived in the community and one of them, an old chief, was soon to provide us with a meal ticket. As I lay in my cot in a temperature of 110 degrees Fahrenheit in the shade, he swept into our hut, and welcomed us. As he grinned, he revealed a few orange-stained teeth that had survived his seventy-three years of life. My father got out a grass mat for him to squat on and then the chief addressed us.

"White woman," he gestured grandly, "I have gifts for you and the little white god. But first I have a request."

"Yes, chief," she replied in her soft, Liverpool accent, as she anxiously eyed the bananas, eggs and the four live, struggling chickens his bearers were holding.

"You must bathe him for me."

My mother knew this little favor would help replenish our dwindling food stocks. He was, for some reason, fascinated to see the "little white god" cleansed of all the clinging dust of Nigeria.

"You must also give me sweet tea with Carnation milk in it," he added.

The tea was served, and Mahma, the houseboy, a strapping giant, one of my mother's first converts to Christianity in the area, filled a bowl of water. Then my mother proceeded to pour a calabash of water over me, time and time again. His wrinkled face beamed with happiness as he watched me being bathed as the smoky fire cast dancing shadows across the room.

After it was over, he ordered one of his servants to "prepare the gifts." He handed them to Mahma, who was forced to chase after two of the chickens that had escaped the attentions of the chief's man. After grabbing both squawking creatures, he wrung their scraggy necks.

"Okay," said the headman to my father, "now I have given you a gift, you must give me one in return."

My father fished about in his short baggy trousers and finally found a British shilling and handed over the coin to the chief. With that the ceremony of "appeasing of the child god" was over. All parties bowed, the chief left as quickly as he had arrived, and our eardrums continued to buzz with mosquitoes.

Mahma became a crowning jewel to my parents. "The local witch doctor was so angry with his conversion that he poisoned his food saying that he had taken the 'white man's religion,'" said my mother. But after three attempts, Mahma did not die so the witch doctor concluded he must be a god, so he left him alone.

"Mahma not only became our cook, but also helped us in evangelism. He would travel with us and carry us across the streams and then go back for the bicycles. He was strong, well built and fearless," my mother said.

"Every Monday he would travel with us and help teach the natives about Jesus. Three boys became Christians under his ministry and built their own church building."

My parents were small in stature, around five feet nothing. Neither had the advantage of wealthy parents to send them to Bible college so they both had to work to earn their tuition. My father attended the Bible Training Institute in Glasgow and my mother attended Redcliffe Missionary Training College in London.

The Beatles were at least fifty years away from formation when my parents were born in Liverpool. Neither had known the other before Nigeria, though my father had attended his wife-to-be's farewell service in the Donaldson Street Gospel Hall, in the shadow of Liverpool Football Club's famous ground in Anfield, in 1937.

It had become a tradition for students who planned to go on to the mission field to attend farewell services around the city and then go to Liverpool's Pier Head to wave off those who were leaving on the huge liners. My father was no exception and he waved Anne off as he had done many others.

She had gone to Nigeria with the intention of teaching the blind in Kano and to do medical work there. Their romance blossomed, however, when they later met at the Minna language school of the Sudan Interior Mission (SIM), and on September 5, 1939 they were married close to the northern walled city of Kano.

Before their marriage, my mother had pioneered a work among the 6,800 blind beggars in Kano, teaching them to read Braille and sharing the gospel with them.

But then, on their marriage, my parents began working at Izom in southern Nigeria among the Yamma section of the Gwara tribe. "These were pagan people, totally different from the Muslims of Kano," she later told me. My parents said that up until my birth, reaching the people had been tough, but the appearance of a white baby changed everything. They were accepted. I would be strapped on a little wooden chair on the front of my father's bicycle and we would bump down seemingly endless dusty trails through nine-foot high grass on either side, which concealed many dangers, from snakes to quiet, watching monkeys. My father would constantly ring the bike's bell to frighten off the wildlife and would be greeted in return by the racket of exotic birds.

He would arrive in a small dusty village of straw-roofed mud huts, and a babbling crowd of near naked people would appear. The sound of the noisy, giggling boys mingled with barking dogs and bleating goats. For those laboring in the fields, the word would quickly go round that "the white god is here," and all work would stop. My father would seize the opportunity to preach to the crowds in the Hausa language.

He also kept their attention by singing, and sometimes playing a 10-inch mouth organ (harmonica). He often carried a large wind-up phonograph strapped to his bicycle, and he would open it and play Hausa hymns on unwieldy 78 rpm records. The crowds would literally fight to put an ear close to the large horn to hear this "strange" music.

When my father was away, my mother would open the dispensary for the patients sitting under a large mango tree in front of our rectangular hut, and try to deal with the many medical problems of the area. Although she had only basic medical training, she was still expected to handle many difficult cases, and even at times was called to amputate gangrenous toes with kitchen scissors.

"As the crowds lined up for treatment, Mahma would preach to them," my mother explained. "He would tell them about the love of Jesus and would often lead them in the singing of choruses. Even after being treated, the people didn't want to leave. They enjoyed the time so much."

Nigeria was, at that time in 1941, still very much a British colony. But this was an area where not too many pith-helmeted civil servants and missionaries had previously ventured. It was a little too far from civilization for most to want to cope with.

But to my parents, it was heaven. My father, especially, had blossomed, as he had never done when he lived in the back-to-back terraced house in Liverpool's crumbling Toxteth district. In Izom he was "somebody." In fact, he became an unofficial judge and was regularly called upon to adjudicate difficult disputes between natives.

"I would sit under the mango tree with most of the village for company and listen to the arguments," he recalled. "Then I would ask the Lord to give me Solomon's wisdom in giving the right judgment or advice. They called me 'Mai hankuri,' which means 'the patient one.'"

As my father dispensed advice and justice, the crowds squatted silently in a semi-circle and I would gurgle contentedly in a swing-chair attached to the mango tree as Jumpa, my African playmate, pulled the rope to keep me moving to protect me from the snakes and mosquitoes. For my parents, the slithering snakes, monster rats, bitter-tasting quinine tablets, the tsetse flies constantly humming around their faces, the debilitating humidity, the hot air that clutched at them like a sauna, the inconvenience of having to constantly boil and filter the water, didn't affect their unquestioning belief that God had called them to this remote area of West Africa.

My mother, a small but outspoken woman made of tempered steel, would regularly do battle with the local witch doctors who dispensed their evil magic. She had no qualms in approaching them about practicing their juju medicine on her patients, something that was illegal under British colonial law. She had been called in several times by natives to try and save the lives of people who had been nearly killed by the evil black magic of the witch doctors.

There were even occasions when my parents would be called to dig up newly-born babies, who had been buried alive by the superstitious natives because the mothers had died in childbirth. The witch doctors had told the people that the evil spirit of the infant had caused the death of the mother and so the baby had to die, too.

Mahma and Baba (another houseboy) would watch in horror from behind a clump of bushes as a burial took place. They would hear the high-pitched shrieking of mourners, and watch the stiff, white-wrapped body of the dead mother being lowered into a freshly dug hole. Then the crying baby, wrapped in a grass mat, was placed beside her, and the hole filled in.

"When all was clear, they would call us to dig up the suffocating child," said my mother. "If the mite was still alive, and most were, we would nurse them and then take them to the mission station at Diko which was run by fellow-missionary, Esther Anderson. There they had a large mission church and Christian women would foster the babies under the guidance of Esther. When they got older, they would be sent to a Christian orphanage and many became nurses and evangelists when they grew up."

She added: "Despite the difficulties, the peace we experienced at the time was indescribable."

Sadly, the happiness was soon to be broken. It began one night when Alf, my father, normally in bed by 8.30, had not arrived home by 9:30. My mother, by the meager light of a storm lamp, was painting scrolls containing Scripture verses and choruses in the Hausa language. Just a stone's throw away my mother could hear the ugly sounds of jackals and hyenas quarrelling. She began to worry. Then she heard a rustle outside, and Alf stumbled in.

"I don't feel...."

His words trailed off and he crashed head first onto the floor. He lay there, shaking, his face contorted in pain. My mother knelt down and took his temperature and discovered it was 103 degrees Fahrenheit. Instinctively she rushed to the dispensary for medicine.

In agony, he rolled from side to side, his pain-lined face streaming with sweat. His brown, curly hair, usually immaculately groomed, was lank and damp. He gazed up at his wife with unseeing eyes. At first my mother recoiled in ill-concealed horror. But then she dragged him across the floor, lifted his pain-racked body onto the bed, and covered him with a mosquito net. She gave him medicine but he couldn't keep it down. He lay in the pale flickering half-light, breathing with difficulty.

What should she do? Her medical knowledge was minimal but it was eighty miles to the nearest hospital. Dropping to her knees in desperation, she cried in a voice barely audible, "Lord, I can't cope. Please help, please...."

Her face was frozen with tension. But suddenly her mind became clear and she took a stick and a storm lamp and ventured through the dangerous bush to the nearest village and called Ungalu, the houseboy, to fetch Mahma and ask him to travel to Abuja with a message for the District Commissioner.

Before Mahma left on his urgent mission, he came and prayed for my father. As he looked down at his pale face, Mahma cried out, "Lord, he that thou lovest is sick."

Mahma discovered that the bicycle he was to travel on had a puncture and my mother had to mend this before he could set off.

A truck was sent and my mother put a camp bed in the back of it, along with some folding chairs, a cot basket for me, and food for us all for the long journey to the hospital at Minna. Along the way, the truck was forced to stop at a broken bridge which had to be rebuilt before we could continue. But finally we made it.

So began the drama that resulted in my father's hospitalization. The doctor discovered that he had the usually lethal combination of malaria, liver disorder and dysentery. The staff at Minna Hospital worked hard to save his life, and after a week of treatment, he began to claw his way back to waking reality.

Soon he returned to us at Izom and was gradually eased back into his routine of making visits to local tribes people, leading Bible studies, and all the duties attached to mission work. For a few weeks he felt fine. Then the malaria returned. It was again followed by liver disorder and dysentery and Esther Anderson treated him at nearby Diko. The cruel tropics were exacting a terrible toll on him, but he struggled on, his emaciated features and yellow skin all pointing to the inevitable fact that Nigeria was no place for him.

My parents had served five years in Nigeria and the time had come for a year's rest, though no one could tell what awaited them in war-ravaged Britain.

3
All At Sea

Tears welled up in my parents' eyes as scores of their African flock gathered outside the compound to say good-bye to us. As we got into the back of an open truck, with our lives packed, lock, stock and barrel into boxes, the people held hands and sang, "God be with you 'til we meet again."

My father remembered the scene well. "The converts ran alongside the truck for at least a mile, waving and saying 'return soon.' The tears just kept flowing from them and us. It was the most moving experience of my life. We really loved those people. We all kept waving until they disappeared in a haze of dust that whirled behind the truck."

After a long journey to the dockside at Lagos, there came a dire warning from a khaki-clad British civil servant.

"Mrs. Wooding," said the grim-faced official, "you may not make it to England. The Germans are sinking ships all the time. You are taking your lives in your hands by making this trip. Do you understand this?"

My mother held me close to her (by now I was a lively eighteen months) and nodded. "I have the choice of either my husband dying here, or of possibly making it to England and getting proper medical treatment for him. He won't last more than another few weeks here anyway. So I have no choice."

With that she carried me up the gangplank of the Dutch passenger ship, *Stuvescent*, and was guided to our cabin by a steward. My father clutched a battered suitcase as he struggled along behind us. Porters loaded a large trunk and several boxes containing our belongings into the hold.

"There are ninety civilian passengers on the ship and the rest are soldiers," announced our Cockney steward. "We are to be part of a convoy of twenty-eight ships protected by four Royal Navy ships. It's going to take a blinking miracle if we all make it back to good old Blighty."

After he left, my parents, in the solitude of the cabin, knelt down and asked for that miracle.

"Please God," my father implored, "May we all make it safely to England. We hand our lives and that of our baby to you. We are completely in your hands."

The sirens sent a chill of horror through most of those on board. My father was about to start a funeral service, which the captain had asked him to perform for an African passenger who had died of black water fever. We were just a couple of weeks at sea when the first German attack came. Everyone had been instructed about what to do if we were hit.

"Get on the top deck. Cut the rope from a lifeboat and take your children, but be prepared to jump into the water," said the weary captain, his voice shrill and strident.

"Why do we have to jump?" one woman, with two children clinging in fear to her skirt, asked in a desperate tone.

"Because, madam, you will have just one minute to get off the ship," he said. He paused then with acute embarrassment added, "We haven't got enough lifeboats to go round. Most of us will have to end up in the sea."

My mother quickly harnessed me into a tiny life jacket and then strapped hers around her body. My father also slipped into his life jacket. For all ninety civilian passengers on our deck there was just one lifeboat. A member of the crew stood poised with a knife in his hand, ready to cut the rope that held that solitary boat. Who got in it was to be anybody's guess. It was going to be everyone for him or herself.

A huge explosion suddenly rocked the whole ship. Then came another and another. It had been as sudden as a cyclone appearing from a clear blue sky. Smoke began billowing from a vessel to the left and also from one in front. Distant screaming filtered through the smoke as hundreds of people leaped desperately from their stricken ships into the heaving Atlantic. There was utter pandemonium.

"Scatter! Scatter!" an urgent voice bellowed from the loudspeaker system. We did scatter, like frightened sheep before a storm. Ships took off in different directions as the Royal Navy escort began the impossible task of fighting off the hidden enemy and trying to rescue survivors from the angry sea. Hundreds drowned in a few minutes.

Our ship shot off with another vessel and after four hours of apocalyptic horror, the captain sounded the "all clear" and announced that the Germans had retreated "for the time being." We were told we could all go to the dining room where a meal would be provided.

All through this I had been oblivious to the danger and was happily running around the deck and through the corridors.

That night brought another order. "Ladies and gentlemen," said the harassed purser, his face bleak, "it is not safe for any of you to sleep in your cabins tonight. I want all the men to sleep in one of the salons and the women and children in another."

My father went to the purser. "Sir," he said in a low voice, "I know you will think that I am crazy, but I have committed this journey to the Lord and I wish for myself and my family to sleep in the cabin."

The man looked in disbelief at the frail figure in front of him, and after a few moments of eye-to-eye dueling, said, "Do you realize that if we are hit, you will not have a chance?"

My father nodded. "Yes, I know that. But I also know that we are in God's hands."

As panic-stricken passengers tried to stave off the fear of death with large quantities of booze, the three of us slept soundly that night.

Next morning, a deputation of passengers came to my father with a request. "Mr. Wooding, please hold an informal service for us." He did this daily for the remainder of the hazardous journey and the room where he held the service was packed to the doors.

For six nerve-racking weeks our convoy of two zigzagged its way from danger. Each morning passengers would rush to the deck to see if our companion ship was still there. Mercifully, it was. Normally the journey from Lagos to Liverpool took only fourteen days. This epic journey meant forty-two days at sea.

I was, however, quite unaware of the dangers afloat. I would spend hours in the barber shop sitting on the swivel chair turning around and around. Sometimes the soldiers would take me to the lower deck where they kept the monkeys they were taking back to Britain, and I would laugh at them as they ran around on their leashes.

From Tabloid To Truth

The sight of the towering Liver Building peeking out through the industrial haze of Liverpool's Pier Head brought a huge cheer from those on board the two ships.

My mother held me close and shouted excitedly, "Danny boy, we're home at last. Thank God, we're home!"

My father's eyes were brimming. He stood quietly thinking of how five years previously he had set sail to Nigeria, with such high hopes, from this very spot. Now he had returned, a physical wreck.

We moved into a semi-detached house in Okehampton Road, Childwall, a pleasant Liverpool suburb, to live with my mother's father Sam, and her sister Ethel. My grandfather, who sported a fine white beard, had been, for thirty years, in both the Royal and Merchant Navy and captivated me with his tales of the sea. I can recall sitting on his lap and listening to endless stories that were as salty as his personality.

Gradually, my father's health improved. He had regular medical treatment at the Hospital for Tropical Diseases in Liverpool. In September 1943, my sister Ruth was born.

After just one year at home, the SIM decided we should return to Nigeria. "But there were no ships available as D-Day was being planned and only troops and men urgently needed for the war effort were allowed to travel," recalled my mother. "They said, however, that Alf could go, but not the rest of us. I was naturally worried as he was still not too well and I wasn't sure he could look after himself in the tropics."

So this "soldier for the Lord" sailed back on a troopship, slept in a hammock, and lined up for grub just like the other fighting men on board.

Back in Nigeria, he felt the all-enveloping peace he had first experienced in the early days of his first term. He moved back to Izom to an ecstatic welcome from the natives there. Then, after a short stay, he moved on to Zaminaka. While there an epidemic of meningitis swept through the area killing hundreds of people. My father was drafted by the British Administration to travel among the natives handing out tablets to try and fight the illness. As he traveled around the primitive villages he was bitten repeatedly by tsetse flies and soon went down with sleeping sickness. That was followed by malaria and then dysentery. He began to shiver, sweat and vomit. Then he experienced terrible headaches, extreme diarrhea and a discharge of blood. He felt completely frustrated.

"Why, Lord" he questioned desperately, "should my missionary future be wrecked by all this illness?" There was pathetic misery in his voice.

A missionary doctor treated him but became more and more disturbed by his lack of physical progress. After more treatment, the attacks just continued and a bitter resentment began to seep into him.

This was compounded when the doctor, peering up from my father's medical records over his half-glasses, told him, "Mr. Wooding, you have no alternative but to leave the tropics for good. I'm terribly sorry."

My mother cried a lot in those days. And she became more and more concerned with each letter she received from him. His spidery handwriting had become very difficult to decipher and she guessed the worst. He must be seriously ill again.

One day she got the news she had been dreading. It came from another missionary staying in Liverpool.

"Anne," she said, her voice hushed, "I think you should prepare yourself for the fact that you will probably never see Alf again. We've had word that he's near to death. I am so sorry."

"Some 800 missionaries in Nigeria," she continued, "have joined in a prayer vigil for Alf. But things look hopeless."

Arrangements were made to put Ruth and me into a home outside of Manchester, while my mother caught the first available ship back to Africa in the hope of seeing him one last time before he died.

Just two days before she was due to leave, a knock came on the door. It was a telegram from an SIM leader in Nigeria, which said, "Don't sail. We have put him on a ship to England. It's the only hope."

Looking like a victim of Belsen, my father finally arrived back in Liverpool and went to Okehampton Road to find that my mother and I were at church. As he walked through the door, Ruth was terrified of him. She ran in fear to her grandfather, wondering who this skeletal figure was.

I can recall returning home and seeing this broken figure

standing there, his hands outstretched for love. I ran to him and he swept me up in his arms.

This return journey had not been as dangerous as the last. The big danger to him now was his terrible health. He was, as one doctor described him, a "museum of tropical diseases."

Gradually Ruth and I began to accept this little man and learned to love him and give him the affection he so needed after such a traumatic experience.

It was back to the Hospital for Tropical Diseases for him, and a period of heart-searching about what had gone wrong. He would spend two weeks in a hospital and then two at home. That went on for twelve long months. Finally, the doctors told him he was cleared of sleeping sickness and plans were again put in motion for our return to Africa.

Just as he was getting his life back together, another grievous blow greeted him. A cable arrived from Dr. Percy Barnden, the doctor who brought me into the world, saying it would be "suicide" for my father to go back.

The African odyssey was over, and he knew it. He would have to find a different way to serve God.

4
Birmingham Blues

The furniture van bumped relentlessly southwards with its sparse cargo of broken-down furniture and the three of us on board. Our destination was Birmingham. It was to be the start of a new life.

As the ninety-mile journey progressed through smoke-caked towns like Crewe, Stafford and Wolverhampton, my mother led us in the singing of Hausa choruses. By now we knew a whole selection by heart. Our voices rose as we passed by factory smoke-stacks spewing black plumes into the air.

My father had already spent three months in this bomb-flat-tened city working with John Wolf, a Hebrew Christian who had established a missionary work to the city's large Jewish popula-tion. Dad had been accepted to work with "God's chosen people" by the Barbican Mission to the Jews (now called Christian Witness to Israel). Mr. Wolf was to move to another part of the city, and my father was chosen to continue this work.

"I'll find somewhere nice for us to live," he had confidently told us as we waved goodbye to him in Liverpool.

"When I've got that place, you can come and join me."

In July 1946 we received the good news that he had secured accommodation and our spirits were sky-high.

"I wonder what my bedroom will be like," I mused aloud.

"Will we have a nice garden, Mummy?" asked Ruth, who by now sported a fine head of light brown curls.

The large green furniture van weaved its way through Birmingham's Bull Ring shopping center. I pointed to the colorful stalls lining the steep cobbled hill that led precariously down from the Bull Ring into Digbeth.

As we drove towards the south of Birmingham I noticed, even as a child, that the city bore terrible scars of war. Everywhere I saw scenes of devastation. Whole streets lay in ruins. Factories, which had once been great, were reduced to rubble and twisted metal. World War Two was now well over, but its black scars were there for all to see. Hitler's Luftwaffe killed 2,241, and many of the survivors would never recover from the mental scars of the blitz.

Although the constant bombing had obliterated large portions of Birmingham, the area we were now in, Balsall Heath, seemed even more run-down and depressing than others we had passed through.

My mother looked at me and held my hand tight. She seemed bitterly disappointed.

"Brighton Road, Balsall Heath. Is that where we have to go to?" the driver asked my mother as we all huddled together in the front seat of the van.

"Yes, that's right; it's number ten." She squinted at the letter my father had sent which had the address on it.

I could see that the cloth-capped driver was as taken aback as we were as he drew up outside a large and extremely drab house that loomed over us like a huge, ugly face.

My mother, with a sick, sinking feeling rising in her stomach, went and knocked at the front door. A woman soon emerged with a cigarette hanging limply from her lips, and sporting a mass of plastic curlers.

"I've got no rooms to let at the moment," she barked, "You'd better clear off."

"No, I'm Mrs. Wooding. I understand my husband has arranged accommodation for us."

"Oh, that's right." She flicked ash on the doorstep. "You've got the attic and another room. You'll have to share the bathroom with someone else though."

Mrs. Reid, a war widow, explained that Mr. Wooding had gone out for the day with Mr. Wolf on a Sunday School outing to Weston-super-Mare. It was by now late afternoon, and she expected him back at any moment.

"I think you should all come in and have a cup of tea, and then I'll show you your rooms," she said magnanimously.

We all trooped into her ground-floor lounge and were introduced to Mr. Mohammed. His thin lips were pulled into a smile that lit up his swarthy face, showing very small, very yellow teeth.

"He's my special lodger," she explained, exchanging a grin with her greasy friend. "He helps keep my spirits up in these terrible times."

The tea arrived, and as we sipped the revolting liquid my father turned up with Mr. Wolf, a dark-skinned man. Obviously flustered, he was full of apologies for being late.

First Mr. Wolf patted me on the head, and then he suddenly lunged at me. "Now, little Danny, I want to kiss you on the cheek." His eyes narrowed. I recoiled in fright. Who was this strange figure bending over me? And what was all this kissing business?

"Why should I let you kiss me?" I was defiant.

"Because I want you one day to tell your grandchildren that you have been kissed by a wolf...."

With that he kissed me on the cheek and threw back his head and roared with laughter.

As we made our way up the uncarpeted stairs that ascended into shadows, I could see my mother and father exchanging words.

"I'm sorry, Nan," [his nickname for my mother] I heard him say, "but I have tramped the streets for weeks trying to get something, and this is the only place I could find that would take children. Things are dreadful here. There is just no accommodation for couples with families."

On his meager wage of three pounds a week, Alf had found life in post-war Birmingham tough beyond words. Hitler's incessant bombing raids had wiped out whole areas. In sheer desperation, he had finally settled for this seedy house in Birmingham's "red light" district.

My mother looked in horror at the state of our accommodation as the smell of decay and rot reached her nostrils.

"Alf," she exploded, "The place doesn't even have electricity. It isn't fit for an animal, let alone a family."

In the main "living room" bugs scuttled up and down the mildewed wallpaper while a few cockroaches fled across the bare floor. A dank piece of flowered linoleum that had probably been in the same place for twenty years, was all that lay between the floorboards and our shoes.

My mother did not mind living in the primitive conditions of Africa, but she had higher expectations in her homeland. She had left before the war, and had no idea how bad conditions would be upon her return.

Aesthetics had a low priority in our new home. "I'm sorry, Nan, but it's the best I could get." My father couldn't be "sorry" enough.

Mother fought back the tears of anger as she discovered the

dingy place didn't even have a cooker; the shared bathroom was appalling, and the bedroom that Ruth and I were to share was an attic with a gaping hole in the ceiling.

"Come on, Mrs. Wooding. It's not all bad," said Mrs. Reid brightly, as she discharged more ash onto the floor.

"There is one problem, however. We have only one gas meter for the whole house. You'd probably be better off using candles."

She paused to take another puff on her cigarette and allowed it to curl into the recesses of her lungs before continuing. "The rent is very reasonable. Only twenty-seven shillings a week."

"But that will hardly leave us enough to live on," my mother protested.

The landlady's mouth twitched.

"Take it or leave it, Mrs. Wooding."

Mrs. Reid was certainly a venomous creature who could turn and sting at the slightest provocation.

On that first night Ruth and I couldn't sleep. The noise of slurred singing from the pub across the road wafted through our window. Suddenly there came the urgent ringing of a police siren. It got louder and louder and was followed by a squeal of brakes.

"It's the cops," I yelled excitedly as Ruth lay cowering under the blankets.

"Let's have a look and see what's happening!"

I pressed my nose to the dirty windowpane and saw, in the dim glow of the moon and nearby streetlight, two women fighting with each other outside the pub. A group of policemen were vainly trying to separate them as they flailed away at each other. Without warning, the spitting combatants suddenly turned on the police and attacked them. Helmets flew as the men tried to stem the scratching tide of hate.

Things got worse when the pub doors shot open and out poured a group of male drinkers who had decided to come to the aid of the women.

"Come on, Ruth," I said hoarsely. "Don't be a scare-baby. Come and watch this. It's really exciting."

By now she was sobbing in sheer terror. She put her hands tightly over her ears, and then hid her face under the pillow.

"It's getting better. There are more police running down the road. Look, there's a Black Maria coming as well. There are about twenty people fighting with the police, but they're winning and pushing them into the van."

Finally her innocent blue eyes peeked out at mine and we almost got the giggles.

For nearly three-and-a-half years those nightly brawls at the Malt Shovel kept me glued to that attic window. It became such a regular occurrence that I didn't wait for the police to arrive. I knew that as soon as "chucking out" time came, trouble was on its way.

To try and keep our minds off violence, my parents arranged for Ruth and me to take piano lessons with Mrs. Helen Price, who played for some services my parents ran, and also to attend missionary rallies at Tennessee, a huge house in the Moseley district, hosted by Mrs. Helen Alexander-Dixon, the founder of the Pocket Testament League. She was the daughter of Richard Cadbury, the founder of the famous chocolate empire.

When my mother was just getting over the initial shock of her new home, she discovered that most of the residents of the house were involved in a variety of criminal activities. Many had false names because they were on the run from the police.

"At first I found Birmingham more difficult to cope with than Nigeria," my mother told me. "The natives in Africa were far more responsive to the gospel and really seemed to love us."

"Mind you, the 'Brummies' had just been through a terrible war and life was hard. That included the rationing of food and clothing. It was a struggle for everyone to keep body and soul together."

Besides trying to find rooms for us, my father had been busy starting up a youth club in a nearby school. About160 children were attending it. He also had a thriving Sunday School there, and had established, with Mr. Wolf, a little Sunday night church service in a rented hall.

Our dreadful accommodation was a constant source of embarrassment to my mother. "What made things worse was the fact that the police often stood across the road from the house and took note of everyone who came in and out," she recalled.

"Your father had by now been ordained as a pastor and wore a dog collar. They probably thought he was a bogus priest or something," she said.

"One day my father and sister Ethel came from Liverpool to stay with us. As they went up the steps, the officers ran across the road and stopped them. They questioned them for several minutes about their reasons for visiting the house. They obviously felt they were up to no good.

"Afterwards, my father said, 'Anne, why are you living in such a dump?'"

"What could I say to him, except, "This is where God has placed us as a family.""

I could tell my father was excited.

"It looks like we've got our own mission hall," he beamed.

"Well, Alf, that's wonderful," enthused my mother.

"It seems," he continued, hardly able to contain his excitement, "the minister of the Sparkbrook Mission in Alfred Street has to leave Birmingham. His wife is ill and needs to move to a better climate. He wants us to take over the place." At last Dad had his own church.

And soon we had our new home. My parents had almost given up hope of ever buying a house for themselves. Through her work serving at a cafe, my mother had managed to save up the huge amount of £200 [about $300] and hoped that this would be enough for a deposit on a house. But when she enquired about a mortgage, the people at the Building Society laughed in her face and said she did not have a hope.

"All we can do is pray," she said firmly. And she did! Every night she would ask the Lord to take us away from those depressing rooms and let us have a proper home of our own.

One day she returned home late beaming with joy. During the summer she often didn't finish until 9.30 p.m.

"Danny, Ruth, Alf, you will be pleased to know that we have, at last, a new home." She stopped to wipe away the tears of joy from her face.

"It's in Kings Heath, a nice area—and kids, the house even has a back garden you can play in."

Heaven had finally arrived for us!

5
Your Dreams Can Come True

My fingers quivered as I counted the morning collection at the back of my father's little wooden mission hall. When I was convinced no one was watching. I grabbed two half-crowns from the collection plate and dropped them into my pocket.

At last I had enough money to get into the St Andrew's soccer ground for at least the next couple of home games. In those days, Birmingham City Football Club had never been as glamorous as their cross-town rivals, Aston Villa, but to me they were everything. I was prepared to lie, cheat and even steal to support them. If I missed a home game, my withdrawal symptoms were painful beyond belief.

As I was congratulating myself that morning on my nifty finger work, my father came over to me.

"Oh, hello Dad," I said casually, hoping he hadn't seen anything. "It's been a good offering this morning. Nearly two pounds [about $3.50]."

"That's funny," he said, adjusting the tight dog collar that seemed to be choking him. "I would have thought there would have been much more than that."

"No, Dad," I lied as convincingly as I could, "that's all there was."

When he returned to his flock, I rubbed my sweating palms together, then felt into my pocket and jingled the two coins that were once again going to be my passport to enter the Small Heath ground to see my idol, goalkeeper Gil Merrick, who played many championship games for England.

I had become a City addict after we had moved to our new house at 5 Featherstone Road, Kings Heath, a middle-class suburb on the southern extremities of Birmingham. But my cash-flow problem was not my only difficulty in those days. The other was my parents opposition to anything they considered "worldly." That included the cinema, rock and roll music, and going to soccer matches. It seemed to me at that time that their motto was, "You name it, we're against it."

"Look, son," my father said one day, "We are not trying to be spoil-sports, but we just don't think a nice Christian boy should be visiting such places. For instance, people gamble on soccer games and we don't agree with that."

"But," I desperately pointed out, "The Blues started as a church team."

"I don't want any more arguments. You are just not going, and that's it!"

With a streak of independence that I had gained from my mother, I decided that their decision was not final and I would go to St. Andrew's anyway. To save further arguments, however, I would carefully cover my tracks so, hopefully, they wouldn't find out.

For each home game, I had another story made up for why I needed to be out all of Saturday afternoon. Standing on the Coventry Road terraces at the west side of the ground on a misty, damp winter's Saturday afternoon, was my idea of heaven. I would shout, scream, and join in the singing of the Blues' anthem, "Keep right on to the end of the road," with the other fanatical supporters.

I lived, breathed and dreamed about soccer. At school, when we were asked to do creative writing about anything we were interested in, I would write about soccer.

"Wooding, you're quite a wordsmith," a teacher at Queensbridge School, Moseley, told me one day. "Have you ever thought of becoming a journalist?"

I shook my head. "I don't think I'll ever get the right academic qualifications to do something like that, sir."

The only subjects I was any good at were creative writing and sports.

"Wooding, don't ever say 'don't' again. If you believe you can become a journalist, you can!"

"Yes, sir," I responded sheepishly, not really believing a word of it.

However, I did begin to write at a more feverish rate. They were usually short stories in which I was the hero.

I would save a penalty shot for the England soccer team against the Hungarians in the last minute of the World Cup final, or score a century for England's cricket team against Australia in a Test Match at Lords.

I also began writing a stream of tongue-in-cheek letters to different periodicals. These "reader letters" were usually completely fictitious.

One I penned as a teenager under the pseudonym of "City Gent" caused something of a storm after it was published in the Birmingham Evening Mail. It read:

> After living in London for six years I have returned to my native Birmingham and am shocked by the drabness of dress displayed by the average Birmingham male. Unfortunately, in Birmingham the businessman, when adorned with his bowler, pinstriped trousers and rolled umbrella, is looked upon as a freak. In London the average city man would feel lost without his battle dress.
>
> Please, Birmingham, let us adopt the smart wear of the Londoner and revolt against the cheap, ugly American-style clothes of today.

One irate reader, "G.E. Jones of Solihull," retorted: "I entirely disagree with 'City Gent,' who wants to put us back to pre-1914."

My first effort at letter writing actually appeared in *The Christian Herald* on September 17, 1949. I was then just eight years old. It was nothing nearly as controversial as the "City Gent" letter and just told of a two-week family holiday in Liverpool.

Despite my limited success as a scribe, my parents were dead-set against my becoming a journalist.

"Look, son," said my father patiently, "we hear that people who work on newspapers drink, smoke and swear. We wouldn't want you involved with people of that sort."

"But..."

"No buts!"

Nervous giggles from thirty girls, pencils already sharpened, greeted me as I walked scarlet-faced into the classroom run by an Irish lady called Miss Mahardy. I suppose being the only boy on such a course for the next twelve months would be some red-blooded male's idea of heaven. To me it was, to start with at least, a time of excruciating embarrassment.

My mother had felt that I was really cut out for office life and so had encouraged me to enroll for a one-year secretarial course at Queensbridge School.

"But, Mum, shorthand and typing?" I protested. "Everyone will think I'm a sissy."

"No, they won't," she said firmly. "And if they do, they will have me to deal with."

I was allowed to skip my fourth year at secondary school altogether, and at the tender age of fourteen-and-a-half years I joined the horde of girls on the school's first-ever secretarial course. I figured that if I ever fulfilled my ambition of becoming a reporter, the shorthand and typing would be important.

But as the course continued, I began to believe it was futile. What kind of life lay ahead of me if I was just a clerk in an office? Surely, I could become a journalist and travel the world.

"No, son, we don't want you to become a journalist," was my mother's abrupt reaction.

"Well, if I can't do that, I'm going to leave school now. I don't want to work in an office all my life." It was now November 1955, and I was, by law, allowed to leave school in a few weeks.

My mother was concerned about the rebellious spirit that I exhibited in regular clashes at home. So, she took me to see the school principal, Miss Marjorie Mason, a large, forceful woman, who took a dim view of my plans for leaving.

"Wooding," she said as she fixed her piercing eyes on mine, "you will never succeed in anything in life if you give up at the first hurdle. If you want to become a journalist, you first have to learn shorthand and typing."

"But, Miss Mason, my parents don't want me to be a journalist."

"Oh," she said, looking at my mother. "Is that so?"

My mother's face became red with embarrassment. "Well... err... we would prefer him to go into a nice office."

"Well," said the principal turning her broad face to mine, "the future lies in your hands. You either leave now a failure or you show your backbone and fight back. And who knows where that will lead? Your dreams may one day come true."

With that I felt I had no alternative but to continue at the school. Her talk had been the jolt I had needed. I had spent too much time lately dreaming, I now had to do something to make those dreams happen.

Months later I stood shaking with nerves outside the principal's office. A messenger had come to our classroom to ask me to appear before her immediately.

I rapped twice at the door of her office in the foyer of the school and her deep voice boomed, "Enter."

She did not look up immediately, but had her nose buried in a pile of papers. After about a minute, in which I felt my heart was about to explode, she looked up.

"Oh, Wooding," she said in a voice that sent shivers up and down my spine. "I have something to say to you."

I gulped.

"Yes, I'm glad you decided to stay on and complete the course. You've certainly worked hard. You've won first prize for the most improved student in the fifth year. Congratulations! Go after that dream."

I was in a daze. Maybe dreams could come true—even in Birmingham!

6
Canada Calling

The airmail letter slid through our Birmingham letterbox
and I quickly scooped it up. I was usually waiting by the
front door for the mail to be delivered, because I had been
engaging in a rather torrid letter-writing campaign with Sharon,
my American penpal in Minnesota.

I certainly didn't want my parents to read any of that ardent
material. But this one had a Toronto postmark on it; so I knew it
must be from Jenny, a friend I had met at a dance that my parents had not found out about.

The letter had arrived just three months after Jenny had headed off to Canada. She was ecstatic about life in this new country.

"Dan," she wrote, "this place is great; much better than grotty
old Birmingham. Why not come over? You'll have a ball."

Toronto. What a thought! I looked it up on the map. It was just
ninety miles from the U.S. border, so I could hop down there regularly and see what America was really like. And, of course, I
would be able at last to meet up with the amazing Sharon.

I switched on the record player in my bedroom and waited for
Rick Nelson's "Poor Little Fool" to drop onto the turntable. I lay
there quietly contemplating my big move. That room itself, with its
bare gas fire and bay window that overlooked our tiny back yard,
had come to symbolize for me that I was very much alone. I had
few real friends and little or no communication with my sister
Ruth, by now a born-again Christian, or my parents.

My thoughts were rudely interrupted when my father thumped
on the door and yelled, "Turn that racket down. It's driving us all
crazy."

The "racket" drowned out my response: "Well, you won't have
to put up with it much longer. I'm off to a better life."

I smiled as I pondered the fact that I would no longer have to
be afflicted with interminable services at the Mission, the clois-
tered center of the universe for my family. There would be no more
days at the boring city-center office where I was working as a

clerk. An approach to the local newspapers for a job had all resulted in the response I had expected; "You do not have enough academic qualifications."

Without telling my family, I took a day off work and caught a bus
to London to visit the Canadian Embassy. There I collected brochures
about life in Canada and discovered the steps I needed to take to emigrate there.

Toronto certainly seemed an attractive proposition and I was in a
consuming hurry to get there. It was an ungovernable urge.

"But you can't leave us like this!" My mother was distraught when
she caught me reading my emigration literature and I confessed that
I planned to leave as soon as the formalities were completed.

"I not only can, but I will!" I said callously. "I've had enough of
you all and God. I'm going to see what the rest of the world is like.
It can't be any worse than here."

It was a sad little group consisting of my parents, Ruth and Aunt
Ethel that, in March 1960, gathered at Birmingham International
Airport to see me off. My father blinked back the tears as he held
me close and said, "God be with you, son. We'll be praying for you."
I nodded, but said nothing. After all, wasn't it to escape the restric-
tions of my parents' religion that I was leaving home?

A lump gnawed at my stomach and my eyes were hot and moist
as I went through to board the small plane that would carry me to
London, where later that day I would catch the connection to
Toronto. There was no turning back.

We touched down in Toronto some eighteen hours later, after a
short refueling stop in Goose Bay, Labrador. The stairs were put
up against the aircraft and I literally ran down them. I was nearly knocked sideways by an icy blast of wind. The formalities were
efficient and polite. A stamp in my passport confirmed that I was
now a "landed immigrant."

The immigration official handed back my passport. "I hope it all
works out well for you in our country," he said, smiling mechani-
cally. "And have a nice day."

I thanked him and then collected my bags and staggered through
customs under the weight of the two cases. As I went through the
barrier, I immediately spotted the composed, mannequin-like figure
of Jenny. We both grinned broadly.

"Well, I've gone and done it now, Jenny," I said as she planted a kiss on my cheek. She could see a look of both excitement and bewilderment on my face.

"Don't worry at all. You're going to love it here."

I wanted so much to believe her, and stammered out my thanks for coming out to meet me. Already gone was her Birmingham accent, and it was replaced with a strange hybrid, which sounded more North American than Brummie.

Over coffee, she began giving me advice on life in Toronto; "By the way," she said casually, "how much money did you bring with you?"

I pulled out my wallet and counted out ten five-dollar notes.

"I make that precisely fifty dollars," I said, holding them up.

Jenny stared, thunderstruck at my naivety.

"You mean to say that's all you've brought to start a new life?"

"Well, it was all I could rake up."

"Dan, are you completely crazy? You'll not last five minutes on that."

I could see she was already beginning to regret giving me the postal hard sell on life in Toronto. We hardly spoke on the bus journey, and then she directed me to the immigration office where I had been instructed to report. As I stood in the gusting, icy, snow-leadened air with the wind clawing at my face, I felt the chill of loneliness envelop me.

Where was the glamour of Toronto that I had expected? All I could see then in 1960 was a few rather feeble skyscrapers, a lot of shabby shops, and cars covered in the filth of the tail end of winter. The city looked even more depressing than Birmingham.

The immigration officer had a bored expression as I sat down opposite him.

"I don't know why you've bothered to come, Mr. Wooding," he said, speaking in a monotone as he tipped back in his chair. "There is a great shortage of jobs here at this time. You'll be lucky to get anything."

With that he told me to return in a few days. He was obviously eager to terminate the conversation, and 1 felt as if I had been hit in the stomach.

I headed out into the biting wind and felt like screaming. Why were people so apparently hostile? What had I done that was so very wrong?

The hotel that I had to check into was like something from an old movie. The decrepit clerk took my government voucher that entitled me to stay free of charge for the first two nights. He picked up my suitcases and wheezed his way up to the second floor where my room was located.

"Don't be surprised if you get a knock on your door during the middle of the night," he grinned toothlessly. "There are some very naughty ladies who like to visit this hotel. Have a nice night!"

I sat on the creaking bed in my small room that had a barracks flavor about it, and turned on the radio. Elvis' "Heartbreak Hotel" came crackling out, and that certainly didn't help my state of mind. I took a deep breath and clenched and unclenched my right fist. I was fighting anger and confusion, and was losing.

What was I doing in Canada? What was I running away from? I was the "Poor Little Fool" that Rick Nelson had been singing about.

I finally undressed. Eventually I drifted off, and slept fitfully.

When I woke next morning I jumped up with a start. I rubbed my eyes and realized I was not in my little room back home, but in a strange and foreign land.

Two days later, I needed to find a new place to live. I managed to get a room at the Central YMCA. It was certainly much better than the hotel, but it did not provide individual radios in the rooms. So I rather foolishly joined the life ebbing and flowing up and down Yonge Street, Toronto's largest thoroughfare, and bought myself a transistor radio.

Then I phoned Jenny. "Hi Dan. How's everything?" She seemed friendly, although I still couldn't get used to her newly acquired North American accent.

"Yes, everything's fine." I paused momentarily, and then added, "Well... except for the fact that I'm broke. I've spent my last dollars on a radio."

"You've what?"

We arranged an urgent meeting and I shamefacedly told Jenny how my fifty dollars had "just disappeared" on food, lodging and the radio.

"You probably think I'm crazy, Jenny, but I couldn't face the loneliness of my room without a radio."

Instead of blowing up, she took, my hand and said gently, "Look, Dan, I encouraged you to come over, so I'll help you all I can. I'll organize a collection at the hostel where I'm staying, and we'll give you a loan. But don't go wasting any more of it."

She had brought a copy of one of Toronto's newspapers, and began searching the room for rent ads.

"We have got to find you an inexpensive place that will give you full board."

I went back to the YMCA canteen and sat and drank my umpteenth cup of tea. I was so low that I seriously considered packing my bags there and then and leaving for home regardless of the consequences. I had run away from my parents and the constant conflicts; also the Mission, but most of all from God. Life as a Christian, it seemed to me, was incredibly boring and irrelevant. But was this any better? I felt like hurling my cup across the room in utter frustration. Then Jenny's voice cut in as she returned from the pay phone.

"Okay, Dan, get packed. I've got you a place to stay," she said, smiling broadly. "It's in the High Park area, which is one of the better parts of Toronto. You'll get a private room and loads of food."

The tram dropped us off at the end of High Park Boulevard, and we began walking down this delightful tree-lined road, full of large detached houses and well-manicured lawns.

"That's yours," said Jenny, pointing to a large solid house. It was red-bricked and had white pillars at the front of it supporting the structure.

Greta, the gracefully slim Austrian "hostess" greeted us at the doorway and showed me my tiny room, which at least was clean and tidy.

The other guests were definitely not friendly. They turned out to be mainly German and they made it obvious to me that an Englishman was not "velcome" in their Teutonic world. No one sat with me at the breakfast table, and they all jabbered away in German in little groups.

Once again a desperate loneliness overwhelmed me. I had, by now, become so low that I would lie on my bed for hours wishing my life would come to an abrupt end. It was an unhappiness I could not handle at all.

Then, five weeks to the day that I had arrived, I finally got a job. The immigration office put me in touch with an insurance company where I was offered the position of accounts clerk at fifty dollars a week.

After two faltering months at the insurance job, I was slowly getting my confidence back, and was even cracking jokes with some of the staff, many of whom were also recent immigrants.

However, I was not prepared for what happened on the Monday of the ninth week when I came downstairs for my breakfast with the Germans. I noticed they were all standing around in agitated groups mouthing Germanic oaths.

"What happened?" I enquired.

"The lady who ran this place has run off with all the downstairs furniture," said one of the exasperated Germans. "Her boyfriend must have come late last night with his van and helped her load it. She's done a midnight flit."

Another added: "I know she was owed back wages by the guy who owned the place, so I suppose she decided to take the law into her own hands and take what she felt she was owed."

So that was it. We were all homeless.

I ran to the nearby pay phone and got Jenny on the line.

"Yes, Dan, what is it this time?" "You'll never believe this...."

"Go on... try me!"

7
Trouble In Toronto

It could have been providence, I don't know. But Alan, the brother of Beth, one of the girls whom I used to see at the lunchtime rock-and-roll dance sessions I secretly attended at the Casino, Birmingham, had arrived in Toronto. He had contacted me and told me that he had moved into what he called a "super apartment."

"Why don't you come and share it?" he suggested on hearing of my predicament.

"There are three of us already, and I'm sure the others wouldn't mind a fourth at all. After all, us Brummies have got to stick together."

We each had our own bedroom, and I got on well with Alan and the others, both Canadians. So with a new base I could begin to enjoy life in Toronto. I found a soccer team to play with, Piccadilly United, and was settling into my job. So it was quite a shock to me when I got home from the office, just six weeks after moving in, and the voluble landlady met me on the doorstep.

"Mr. Wooding." She was obviously in a serious mood. "I am sorry to tell you that there has been a complaint against you by the others," she said in a sharp, accusing tone.

"Complaint?"

"Yes, I'm afraid they feel you haven't been doing your share of the washing up."

I broke into a chuckle.

"But that's not true. Well, I may have missed on a few occasions."

"I don't want to argue with you," she cut in. "I just want you to pack up your things and leave. I'm giving you one week's notice to find somewhere else to live."

She wasn't joking as I had first thought, and I was numb with shock. The others were quite embarrassed with the situation, but obviously they had got together and decided that for some reason they wanted me out. They already had somebody else to take my place.

As I went to my room, I found a letter waiting for me from my mother. Since I had arrived in Canada, she had bombarded me with endless airmail epistles. Mostly they were snippets about life at the Mission.

"Everyone is praying for you there," she wrote this time. I usually skipped quickly past these parts of the letters, but I couldn't ignore her comments about my father's health, all apparently resulting from his problems in Nigeria.

"He's been in poor health," she said. "I don't know how much longer he will be able to continue at the Mission. I think things are more serious than he lets on."

Fortunately, that night I had a soccer game for Piccadilly United. I hoped that would help lift the gloom. During half-time I mentioned to the rest of the team that I was in desperate need of a new place to live.

Jack Loughran, our Ulster-born right-winger, came over to me.

"Dan, I've got room in my basement flat. Why don't you move in with me? We can share the rent. What do you say then?"

"What can I say, but thanks! Can I move in tonight?"

Life with Jack, a kindly bachelor in his early thirties, was a pleasure. He was a Roman Catholic who was extremely tolerant of other views. He loved sports and pop music, as I did, so we got on very well.

With the constant pressure from my mother to start going to church again, I thought I had better make a few token visits to keep her happy. One Sunday, I listened to a live service from the People's Church on the radio, and I decided to go there the following week.

I caught the subway and made my way into the old building that then housed the church. I felt a strange glow that morning as I heard old, familiar hymns again. I had actually brought along the Bible that my mother had given me at Birmingham Airport and I followed the Scripture reading.

The preacher looked like an Old Testament prophet with his long white flowing locks. He was Dr. Oswald J. Smith, a world-famous preacher whom Billy Graham once described as "the greatest combination pastor, hymn writer, missionary statesman, and evangelist of our time." I cannot remember what Dr. Smith spoke about that morning, but I can remember being astonished that he issued a morning "altar call." Many people went to the front of the church to accept Christ.

As I watched, I could almost feel my white-haired mother squeezing my arm and whispering as she had done on many occasions before, "Go forward, son. Now's your chance to get right with the Lord." But I wouldn't. My pride wouldn't allow it.

Sunday after Sunday I joined the large congregation at the church. During one service, two robed members of the choir actually came from their seats to decide for Christ.

That took real courage, something I didn't have. They had publicly admitted they had been living a lie.

Jack used to get on to me and ask, "Dan, why do you keep going to that church?"

I told him I didn't really know, but that there was something special going on there and I was hoping some of it would one day rub off on me.

After eleven months in my job my departmental boss, Chuck, called me over to his desk.

"Well," he paused as if not quite knowing how to phrase what he had to say. "You see... well look, there's been a complaint against you," he continued, tapping his foot nervously.

"Complaint?" I was mystified. "Haven't I been doing my share of the washing up then?"

He looked puzzled. "No," he said acrimoniously, "it's just that some of the girls here say that you need to take a bath a bit more often."

"Smelly?" I was shocked and hurt at being labeled such a villain. "Yes, they feel you should clean up your act and start using a more powerful deodorant."

He paused to allow his words to sink in.

For a moment I sat there blinking, not totally comprehending what he had said. Then an angry flush began to climb up the back of my neck. Why, I thought, should I take this from these silly people?

"But this place is like a sauna. You have the heating far too high... and...."

Chuck raised his hands to try and forestall my torrent of rage.

My voice rose three octaves as I shouted, "Okay, Chuck, I'll just go and have three showers, one after the other. Is that okay with you?" In the heat of anger I stood up and addressed the office. "Is that okay with all of you?" I yelled.

That night, Jack and I began discussing our respective complaints about Canada over a few drinks.

"I can't see what I'm doing here, Jack. They say at work that I stink. Well, I think this whole place stinks. They treat you like you're a criminal rather than someone who has come to help build their country."

"Now, hold on, Dan. Canada's been good to me."

He could see I was just about all in. "Don't you think you've had enough to drink tonight, Dan? Sleep on it. You'll probably feel better in the morning."

At times like this that I began to wonder what on earth I was doing in Canada. For much of the time, I was consumed with intense loneliness. The weather didn't help either. The summer was hot and sticky and the winter was seemingly never ending.

That night, I lay in the darkness, breathing heavily, waiting for honest sleep to blot it all away. It didn't. For next morning, another letter came from my mother. I groaned as I ripped it open, knowing that it would contain at least three sermonettes.

But this time, it didn't!

"Dan, your father collapsed while preaching at the Mission last Sunday and the doctor says that he thinks he's got cancer. "If you feel you can, please come home quickly. It may be the last chance to see your dad alive."

There was a pathetic urgency in her tone. What should I do? I felt conflicting emotions: sadness for my father, and anger with Canada, an anger born of frustration and humiliation. But if I returned home, I knew I would have to admit that I had made a mess of my decision to move to Canada. But still, there seemed little alternative.

With shaking hands I picked up the phone and dictated a cable to my mother. It said, "I'll be home as soon as possible. Love, Dan."

The icebergs from our windy vantage point at the rail of the *Empress of Canada* looked both menacing and magnificent. A flock of seagulls stood motionless on one of them.

Jack looked vacant. "Dan," he mused, "what have you got me into? Life was safe in Toronto. Now you've got me sailing back to England to start all over again."

Our regular conversations back at the apartment had resulted in our making a joint decision to leave Canada and head back to England. I would naturally go to Birmingham, and he would try his luck in London.

"I suppose," he conceded, "I had got into something of a rut. But life was safe."

I knew that I, too, was taking a risk by heading back home. I would have to swallow my pride and start attending services at the Mission again. I guessed that people I had known would label my emigration attempt as a disaster and, to a great extent, it was.

But really I was going home out of a sense of guilt. I could not have remained in Canada while my father was so ill. He was going through a real nightmare. Because of his past record of tropical illness, he had been making regular visits to see a consultant at a Birmingham hospital. The doctor had conducted a series of tests over a period of months. He wanted to discover why my father was always in such pain and why he suffered constantly from diarrhea. It was during one such visit that the specialist had finally told him, "I'm afraid you have cancer."

The shock was like a knife that drove deep into his mind. He sat there stunned, trying to take in what the specialist had said.

"We'll have to operate on you," added the doctor. "Otherwise, you've got a maximum of three months to live."

My father stumbled from the hospital towards the bus to take him home. How could he break such terrible news to his wife and Ruth? He climbed on board, paid the fare and withdrew into himself. He sat there, unaware of his surroundings, praying silently: "Lord, not cancer. Please, not cancer."

Mother knew something serious was up when he walked through the door. She brewed a cup of tea and said, "Come on, Alf, what's wrong?"

The whole story came tumbling out. She was stunned, yet she knew the strain of his years of illness could not go on forever and was relieved that something was to be done.

"Never mind, Alf. There is a scripture that talks about everything working together for good to those who love God. I believe that, and you must too."

Her eyes held his. "Anyway," she said gently. "I believe this news will mean that Dan will be home soon and we'll see a big change in him."

"Maybe..." he smiled weakly. "Maybe...."

8
The Prodigal Returns

The Liver Building rose up majestically in the silent, muffled world of white, salty, drifting fog of that Liverpool morning. There was a damp sting in the air as I stood peering through the mist at the crowds of people excitedly waiting dockside, and as the crew began to tie up the *Empress*, the white-haired figure of my mother, came into view. She was with the more substantial form of her sister, Ethel, and they were both waving madly at me. I felt tears well up in my eyes as I waved back.

I was home!

A motherly hug greeted me as I tumbled through the exit of the rather shabby customs shed. "Hi. How is Dad? Is he still alive?" There was a big lump in my throat.

My mother looked frailer than I had ever seen her. Her face was milk white, but her still gray-blue eyes locked onto mine. They were as steady as ever. "He's very ill. But your coming back will really buck him up."

I introduced Jack to her and then he headed out for his new life in England.

My favorite aunt, Ethel, then greeted me with a kiss. Later, when my mother was out of earshot, she said, "Dan, you've done the right thing. Your parents have been pining for you. You don't know how much they have missed you."

"But," I said mystified, "I caused them so much trouble."

"Yes," she explained patiently, "but you are still their son and they love you."

My father looked gaunt, but managed to smile as I came into the living room. He was wearing a dressing gown and shakily got to his feet as I walked in. He seemed unsure as to whether he should hug me or just shake hands. He settled for a gentle handshake.

"Welcome home, son," he said, his lips pale and quivering with emotion. "I've really missed you. You'll find your rock-and-roll records are a bit worn out, but otherwise your room is still the same."

I looked at him, a quizzically.

"Do you mean to say you've been playing my records? But you hated them!"

He allowed a thin smile to pass over his face. "When you left, I missed you so much that I would go up to your room and play the records and imagine you were still here. I liked Pat Boone the best."

I couldn't hold back any longer. "Oh, Dad, I can't tell you how much I've missed you and Mum."

A week before Christmas, 1961, my father was admitted to the Queen Elizabeth Hospital in Birmingham. It was life or death for him. The cancer would have to be cut away.

We visited him daily and, each time, before we left home, my mother and Ruth implored God to help him. I sat quietly looking on, but not participating. One day, just before the operation, I broke down. "Mum," I sobbed, "I'm not worthy to ask God to heal Dad." I had reached the point of desperation.

At his bedside on the morning of the surgery, I felt like weeping again. The lines of strain around his mouth showed more than ever. His cheeks had become hollow with the skin taut over his facial bones. He was thin enough for me to see the recoil of his heart after each beat. He looked so tired, so close to eternity. But as I gazed at his face, integrity was etched into every line. His faith was still strong. That was important to me.

"Dan," he said in a tremulous voice as his weak, white-knuckled hand gripped mine, "thank you for coming home." His voice was very low now, hardly audible. "I may not come out of this alive, but whatever happens, I hope we will meet again, in heaven." He tried to say more but his voice would not cooperate. I stood there for a few long moments. There were no words, but the communication was total.

With that, he was wheeled into the operating theatre, not knowing if he would come out alive and I experienced the stabbing pain of guilt. With a feeling of helplessness, I watched my father's slight figure disappear down the corridor in an almost funereal way.

The ward nurse told us sympathetically that it would be a long operation, and we should go home and wait.

"Maybe," she said gently, "you could phone in about six hours. It should be over by then."

When we arrived home on that icy winter's day, I headed straight up the stairs to my bedroom. The barn-like room was freezing and I inserted sixpence into the gas meter and then lit the fire. I felt unable to talk to Ruth and my mother. I needed solitude.

As I paced the room, tears began to tumble down my flushed cheeks. I had run away like the prodigal son in the Bible. I had caused much pain to my parents, and now my father was facing death and I knew I might never see him again.

"Lord, I don't want to say good-bye forever to my Dad," I beseeched God as I prowled around like a caged tiger.

Suddenly the air seemed crammed and vibrating with electric potential and my weak ankles almost buckled. Without thinking, I sank to my knees at my bedside and cried out my apologies to God for all the wrongs I had done in my twenty years of life. My breath wrenched out of my lungs in painful sobs. In the stillness, my heart was beating audibly in my ears.

"Lord, I believe, I really believe in you." I wiped away the tears with my gray woolly sweater before I could continue.

"I don't know if I will see my father again in this life but, please, I want to see him again in glory.

"Forgive me for my rotten, selfish past. My temper, my anger, my pride and rebellion. Please wash away my sins and, please...please, take over my life.

"Use me and, if it is your will, please spare the life of my Dad."

I must have been on my knees for half an hour. Finally, I rose to my feet and walked unsteadily into the bathroom and threw cold water on my face to wash away the tears. Then I slowly closed the door behind me and went downstairs where my mother and Ruth were deep in conversation. All at once I wanted to laugh and cry and to shout aloud.

"What's up, Dan?" called my sister timidly, seeing my blotchy features. "You look as if you've been crying. That's not like you."

"Well, I've gone and done it. I asked Jesus to forgive me and come into my life."

They both looked stunned.

"Cheer up, Mum," I added, a smile appearing on my tear-stained face, my eyes gleaming. "It could have been worse. I could have gone forward at one of those awful Youth for Christ rallies you used to drag me along to at the Town Hall." With that I pulled a mock, stern face.

Her tense face visibly relaxed as she got the joke! We all broke into unrestrained laughter and then threw our arms around each other. We were not an emotional family, but we all felt this was a time to let it all out! The pent-up emotion released itself at last. As I laughed out loud I realized how little joy there had been in my life over the past year.

Time seemed to fly as we, at last, had this bond of being a united Christian family. Ruth had made her commitment to Christ some years previously. Words of joy gushed out from all of us.

I suddenly glanced at my watch and said, "Come on, Mum, let's go to the phone box down the street and call the hospital. Surely, they'll have some news for us."

The three of us put on our coats and headed out into that Birmingham winter's night to the call box.

Ruth and I were standing in the icy wind, swinging our arms against the cold as my mother made the call and the nurse came on the line. I could see the slight color rise in my mother's cheeks as the conversation continued.

"He's survived the operation and is back in the ward," she said with tears brimming. "The nurse says he's very weak but, praise God, he's alive."

"Thank you, Jesus," I yelled. Somehow this type of language, which had once made me shudder, now seemed right. I felt intensely alive.

"Thank you, Lord!"

As we walked home, I said to Mum, "I saw your cheeks redden as you said something on the phone to the nurse. What was it?"

"Tell him," my mother answered, "our Prodigal has finally come home. He'll understand."

I felt a choking sensation in the base of my throat, and again the sharp sting of tears.

9
Our Norma

It was hard for me to take my eyes off the raven-haired beauty who sat engrossed in her accounting books at the other side of the glass partition that divided our offices. She had short black hair, a thin elegant nose, and large brown eyes. Her delicate olive-skin face had a hint of Latin about it.

We had met in the far-from romantic surroundings of a company that manufactured little dynamos for bicycle lights. It was housed in a crumbling building in the Aston district of Birmingham. Jobs were hard to come by in the early 60's in this city. I had been to a labor exchange to discover what jobs were available, but I didn't exactly get off to a good start. I had held out my hand to the officer there and he had studied it as if it were some dubious foreign object.

"What would you really like to do?" he finally asked, trying to sound chatty.

"I'd like to be a journalist," I said brightly, hoping he would immediately phone the *Birmingham Evening Mail* and arrange an interview for me.

He offered a dry smile and peered through his rimless glasses at my qualifications which showed I could type and I had learned shorthand, and that was just about it.

"Well, son," he said tonelessly, trying to stifle a yawn and shuffling the papers in front of him, "I would think the best I could do for you with these qualifications is get you a job as a clerk in a factory. It pays ten pounds a week. How does that sound to you?"

I looked at him sharply. He looked back levelly. The "job" he had in mind meant that I would be earning less than when I left for Canada some twelve months earlier. Nevertheless, I contemplated the opportunity he presented. It was as if God was telling me that I must now start out on a pilgrimage and, although some of it would not be pleasant, I was to be patient and obedient and learn to walk with him. Wherever he led me, I must go.

I got the position and the bus journey from Kings Heath, with a change in the city-center, took an hour. I would use the time to read my Bible. Being brought up in a Christian family meant I knew the Scriptures quite well, but they had never come alive for me before.

During a particularly tiresome journey I fluttered the pages of my black leather-bound Bible and my eyes rested on the story, in Genesis, about the creation of Eve.

I read in Genesis 2:20—"The man gave names to all cattle, and to the birds of the air, and to every beast of the field; but for man there was not found a helper fit for him."

I read on: "Therefore a man leaves his father and his mother and cleaves to his wife, and they become one flesh" (verse 24).

As I closed my Bible, completely oblivious of the people sitting around me talking or reading a morning paper, I began to pray silently.

"Lord, you know how lonely I've been over the past years; it's been terrible. Now I realize that I need a 'helper' to be with me so that we can serve you together."

My mother had constantly been trying to interest me in girls who came to the Mission, but none of them had really taken my attention.

Now Norma, the slightly built raven-haired girl who sat behind the glass, was different.

"Is she the one for me, Lord?" I asked on the bus. "If so, please give me the courage to ask her out."

For nearly two months I tried to speak to her. But somehow the words would just dry up in my throat.

"Lord," I said quietly in the office one day, as the typewriters clattered, "I need courage now. Show me what to do."

I went to the antiquated adding machine in another office to total the day's orders, and found Norma sitting at another accounting machine inputting data. I tried to make desultory conversation, but again I froze. My knuckles went white with tension. But eventually I was able to speak.

"Norma." She turned and looked at me. Her skin was radiant, her eyes bright.

"You have the sort of face only a mother could love."

My nerves had caused me to repeat something that a friend had once said to me at school. I don't know why, unless, of course, the Lord had a sense of humor.

There was a moment of shocked silence and then she responded, "I beg your pardon."

I put my hand over my mouth to cover my embarrassment.

Then I did it again. "Norma, that's what I like about you—NOTH-ING!"

Her eyes met mine, and both of us got the giggles. The tension had gone and I was still chuckling as I returned to my desk.

I reached into my briefcase and pulled out some writing paper and began forming a letter to her. She has kept it to this day. It read:

Dear Norma,

> Hi! As I am a bit of a coward in asking nice girls for dates, I wondered if I could ask you, through this letter, if you would do me the honor of coming out with me tomorrow night or, if you can't make it, then one night next week.
>
> I have been wanting to ask yo out for a long time but didn't quite know how to do it, so at last I have decided to ask you and I do hope you will say yes!
>
> If you do say yes, can you let me know where you would like to go (any place you like) and it shall be arranged.

I slipped into her office and while she was talking to another girl and left it on her desk. The envelope said, "To Our Norma."

I felt a flush spread across my cheeks as she looked at me shyly through the partition. "Yes," she mouthed, her eyes glistening. "I'll go out with you. I thought you'd never ask."

We went to see a film the next night at the Odeon Cinema in New Street, Birmingham. We had to wait for an hour in the pouring rain and when we finally got inside, there were no double seats left and so we had to sit apart for the film, which was about homosexuals. We both laughed about such a bizarre start to our relationship.

After we got back to her terraced home in Aston, not far from where rocker Ozzy Osbourne was born, we were about to kiss goodnight when he father came out and shouted, "Norma, come inside right now." She quickly went inside and I ran to get my bus back home. What a start to our relationship!

"Lord," I said as the late-night drunks staggered on and off the bus at each stop, "I want to thank you for my future wife. I am now going to open my Bible again, and I would ask you to speak to me through it."

I just rustled the pages of the pocket-sized Bible and came to

John 15:7, "If you abide in me, and my words abide in you, ask whatever you will, and it shall be done for you."

"Lord," I whispered, "I asked for a helpmate, and you gave me one tonight. I accept that verse as your confirmation."

I spent most of my spare time with Norma, and even went back to her home at lunchtime to eat my corned-beef sandwiches and to talk with her parents, Howard and Maud. However, I found it almost impossible to share my faith with her.

One day we were walking along hand-in-hand when we passed a Gospel Hall with the sign prominently displayed, "God so loved the world that he gave his only begotten son."

"I used to go there to Sunday School," Norma remarked as her voice wavered a little. "I loved it."

Then she looked quizzically at me. "Aren't you religious, Dan? I've seen you reading your Bible at your desk during the break." Her eyes held mine steadily.

"Yes, well not exactly religious. I'm a Christian. There is a difference!"

She squeezed my hand affectionately and said, "Tell me about it. How did you become a Christian?" There was a rapt attention on her face as she turned her eyes on mine.

Out poured the whole story of my rebellion, my trip to Canada, my intense loneliness, and my father's illness, from which he had made a remarkable recovery.

"My dad's doing fine, really fine," I assured her. "He's now back doing a little preaching at the Mission, where he's the pastor."

"But why won't you introduce me to your parents?"

"I will—one day. But I didn't want to put you off."

I had to admit that although I had asked the Lord to find me this wife, I still feared she would ditch me if she thought either me or my family were "religious nuts."

After taking Norma out for two months, I bought myself a Lambretta scooter. We would go out together on it, and on Sunday nights I would ride from the evening service to her home.

I also used it for work each day. But, as I was to discover to my cost, scooters can be lethal in frosty weather. One night, returning home from Aston, I found myself driving through tendrils of freezing mist, as white and fine as floating lace. Too late I saw a red traffic light and hit the brakes. As if in slow motion, the whole machine slid away at the back and I crashed headlong onto the road. Fortunately, there was no other traffic around and I was wearing a helmet, so my head was protected. But as I hit the ground I felt a dart of pain in my left leg. It was lacerated and bleeding. I managed to get back on the machine, start it, and gingerly drive it home.

After my mother cleansed my wound, I asked Dad to do me a favor.

"I expect you've guessed that I have a girlfriend at work. She's lovely. Her name is Norma. I wonder if you would phone her tomorrow and tell her what's happened. Explain that I'll be away for a few days."

"Of course I will," he said gently. "Why don't you invite her over?"

The next night Norma sat at my bedside clasping my shaking hand. My parents fussed around her, and my sister and Norma hit it off immediately. When we were alone, Norma turned to me and said, "Your family isn't the slightest bit strange as you led me to believe. I'd like to start going to the Mission with you."

"Done!" We shook hands on the deal.

Our wedding took place on July 13, 1963, at Aston Parish Church. We could have been married in the Mission, but with so many friends and members of the family wanting to attend, we felt the little hall would not accommodate so many people.

It was a beautiful occasion, without any hitches. But as we sped away on the train to Babbacombe, Devon, I had an uneasy feeling that something was not quite right with our relationship. What could it be? We loved each other and could hardly bear to be apart.

The green fields outside the window were just a blur as the train raced west. Norma took out a novel to read. Strangely enough it was *From Here to Eternity*.

"Lord," I whispered, "please show me what is wrong. I don't understand why I feel so uneasy."

As Norma's eyes were glued to the novel, I got out my Bible and opened it at 2 Corinthians and my eyes stopped at verse fourteen of chapter six. There I read, "Do not be mismated with unbelievers. For what partnership have righteousness and iniquity? Or what fellowship has light with darkness?"

I closed my Bible and allowed those words to sink into my mind. I was confused. Although I was convinced that God had brought us together, I knew Norma was not a believer in the way the Bible taught. I felt the Lord was saying to me, "Yes, I did bring you together, but you will never be able to serve me properly until she, too, has committed her life to me."

I leaned over to Norma and asked, "Darling, are you a Christian?"

She looked up puzzled from her book and threw a quick, startled glance at my face.

"That's a funny question to ask on our honeymoon," she said after a long moment of awkward silence. "Of course I am. I love going to the Mission and I say my prayers at night."

"Yes, I know all of that, but the Bible talks about being 'born again.' Have you had that experience?"

"Well, no..." her voice trailed off.

We had this conversation several times during the rain-splashed week of our honeymoon in Babbacombe. Even as we gingerly lay cradled in each other's arms on the squeaky bed in our hotel room, we talked incessantly about what a living faith really was.

"I don't know if I'm ready yet," she admitted one day as we huddled under an umbrella gazing out over the beautiful rain-lashed cliffs. "Just don't put the pressure on me. If you really do believe in prayer, pray for me that I might find what you keep talking about."

One day after we arrived back in Birmingham, Norma suggested we ought to visit her parents and give them the gifts we had bought for them in Babbacombe.

"Then we'll go and see Hilda and Joe," she said. Norma had already told me of her great affection for this couple that lived close by.

"Hilda became my second mother," she told me. "I used to confide in her all the time. I would have dinner with her and her Welsh-born husband, Joe, on Sundays. It became a tradition."

Hilda was a professional dressmaker and had lovingly spent many hours making Norma's beautiful wedding dress. As we pulled up on my scooter outside Norma's family home, she removed her helmet and said, "Do you know that Hilda told me at the wedding that that day marked the end of an era. She said, 'Norma, you'll never have Sunday dinner with us again.'"

I knocked at the front door of their house and Norma's mother

Maud answered it. She looked gaunt. Her eyes were dark from many tears.

"What on earth is wrong, Mum?" asked Norma. "Come and sit down. I've something to tell you."

I joined Norma on the settee and squeezed her hand.

"What's up?" Norma was impatient.

"Hilda's dead."

"What!"

"She died in a car crash in Wales the day after your wedding. Joe's still in hospital with serious injuries."

Norma was numb with shock, at first unable to respond. She covered her eyes with her hands and began to weep deep, heartfelt sobs that shook her whole body.

"Oh, my God, not Hilda...." Her face was bleak. I tried to console her, but it didn't help. It was a terrible moment. She looked at me with stricken eyes, and in the hysteria of the moment ran her hands through her hair.

That night, in bed in our new home on the upper two floors of my parents' house, she clutched me tight in the darkness with a fierce, panicky tightness.

"Dan," she said, her eyes dark-circled and tear-streaked. "Why has God allowed such a thing to happen? Why? Why?" There was desperation in her voice as she moaned in protest at the loss of her dear friend.

I kissed her tears. "Maybe the Lord is slowly knocking away the props in your life so you can really trust only in him."

10
Through Gates Of Splendor

U sually it was not difficult to find a seat at the Mission, but this Sunday night was different. Of course there were the usual "missioners," but the place was also full of young people I had not seen before. Most wore sashes that were inscribed with the words, "Ribbons of Faith." They were from the Sparkbrook Elim Pentecostal Church and had been invited by my father to take the service.

Norma smiled eagerly. I knew she felt they would certainly make a colorful alternative to the succession of dour middle-aged preachers who had been occupying the pulpit to lighten my father's still-fragile shoulders.

After eighteen months of marriage, we had settled down to a relatively comfortable life. By this time I had left the cycle generator company and was earning the princely sum of fifteen pounds a week with an electrical company in the Hockley district of the city. Andrew, our first son, had been born, and everyone agreed he was the "spitting image of his father."

Norma was well accepted by the regulars at the Mission. In fact, no one even questioned that she wasn't a Christian. She knew the strange lingo that evangelicals speak, "the language of Zion," and could mouth all the acceptable phrases.

But there was still uneasiness between us. I didn't want to force her to make that final commitment, remembering all too well my own negative response to my mother's pressures at the Youth for Christ rallies held in the Birmingham Town Hall.

In the pulpit was Adrian Hawkes, a cherub-faced young man who led the "Ribbons of Faith" outreach team. He cleared his throat and explained to our mainly aging congregation, that their group had been formed so they could "reach out with the gospel to the people of Birmingham."

He said in his slight Birmingham accent, "Jesus' great commission in Mark 16:15 was, 'Go into all the world and preach the gospel to the whole creation.'"

Adrian said the command from Jesus, "isn't an optional extra; it's something all Christians have to do. I challenge you here tonight to join with us in evangelizing this city for Christ."

As he spoke I felt my face stiffen a little.

My sister Ruth, who was home for the weekend from her Teacher Training College in Lancashire, came over to me after the service.

"Dan, that was a great challenge," she said full of enthusiasm. "Let's go and talk to Adrian and see how we can help."

The young preacher suggested we should go along that night to their "Late Night Special," which took place each Sunday evening in the back hall of their church.

"Anything can happen at these meetings," he warned. "Most of our clientele are bikers in black leather. So be prepared for a shock. What we are doing is not easy and there can be violence."

There was! But still the group shared the gospel with the noisy, heckling bikers who jeered, cheered and whistled, especially as the girls sang. And as the sermon was preached, Neanderthal grunts came from all over the room, and it quickly turned into bedlam.

"It's pretty wild in here," I breathlessly whispered to Ruth, who had been deep in prayer for the team.

"Yes," she nodded, "this is a whole different world from the comfortable rallies we are used to."

As we left, Ruth and I discussed what we had seen, and what we had been challenged to do. We agreed this was real frontline evangelism. Then an idea began to form in my mind.

"Why don't we start our own work at the Mission?" I suggested as my voice wavered a little.

"But we hardly have any young people," said Ruth.

"There's you, me and Norma... and that's about it." I nodded.

"Well, if the Lord is in this, he'll supply us with the 'troops' we need," I said. "Otherwise this will never get off the ground."

A few days later we met at my home with Adrian and a few of his leading evangelical "storm troopers." I told them that we wanted to form a team called the Messengers, and felt we should start with a coffee bar in the back hall of the Mission on Saturday nights. Adrian agreed to back us and I also made contact with Jim Harding, Director of Evangelism at the Birmingham Bible Institute

(BBI), and he promised to commit some of his students for the first few Saturdays.

So, on a freezing January night in 1965, a group of about thirty of us began transforming the back hall into a coffee bar. There was a time of prayer and then teams went out in twos into the frost-laden streets of Sparkbrook to invite people to the meeting.

I stayed behind at the Mission to welcome them. We had prepared lots of steaming coffee, and a gospel group from another church was to supply the music. We had also rented a slide presentation on five American missionaries slain in January 1956 by Auca Indians in Ecuador. Adrian Hawkes was to preach.

I hadn't expected any of the older members of the church to attend that first night, so I was surprised to see the frail figure of Elsie Budd shuffling in and leaning heavily on her stick as she eased her way towards us.

"I'm sorry I'm late," she apologized breathlessly, "but the icy pavements meant it has taken me longer to get here than usual."

I looked, at this behatted old lady, someone who in my teenage years had often provided me with Sunday lunch, and could have wept.

"But you shouldn't be out on a night like this," I protested.

She looked gently at me.

"Dan, do you remember in Ezekiel 22, where the Lord had decided to destroy the land? It says in verse thirty, 'And I sought for a man that should stand in the gap before me for the land, that I should not destroy it: but I found none.'"

I nodded.

"Well, you see, I've come to 'stand in the gap' for you. I may be too old to talk to these young people who will be coming in, but I can pray while you and your friends are sharing Jesus."

Soon people started coming in and the meeting began. There were none of the troubles of the "Late Night Special," and Norma began serving coffee to everyone in the room.

She came and stood by me as the slide presentation on the murdered missionaries began. We clasped hands tightly as at the end when a picture of the five martyrs was flashed on the screen. It showed them gathering around a tape recorder before they were killed and singing "We Trust in Thee."

Aucas speared them to death shortly after making this actual recording. There was a hushed silence as lights came on. I could see that Norma had been particularly moved by their story. Then Paula, a student from the BBI came over to ask Norma to accompany her to a nearby coffee bar. Paula and her husband Keith headed for the door and I squeezed Norma's hand reassuringly.

As I stood on the steps of the hall and watched them leave, I prayed that something great would happen to Norma that night.

At the Ladypool Road coffee bar, Norma listened with rapt attention as Paula shared her faith simply and sincerely. On their way back to the Mission, Paula turned to Norma and asked her earnestly, "Have you ever given your life over to Christ?"

She hesitated for a moment. "Well, not exactly, but I do pray and go to all the services with Dan. I think I'm a Christian."

"It's no good to just think you are a Christian. You have to know! You have to have an assurance that you have made your peace with God.

"Let's go back to the Mission right now and you accept Christ into your life there."

"Okay... I'll do it," she said, after a long moment of awkward silence.

They slipped back into the sanctuary and Norma asked God to forgive her sins and then invited Christ into her life.

We were clearing up after our outreach, and as Norma entered the room I could see by her shining eyes that something had happened to her.

Paula whispered in my ear, "Dan, your wife has something to tell you."

"Yes, love," I said as I began putting chairs back in place for the Sunday School next morning.

"I've done it... I've been born again by Jesus. I'm a Christian," she said in a husky voice. Her lower lip quivered with emotion and there was a flush on her high cheekbones.

I took her in my arms. "Norma, this is the happiest moment of my life. Now we can work together in whatever God has in mind for us." Little did I know what he had in mind for us at that time!

11
Junkies Are People Too

The doctor from a local drug clinic was being interviewed on a TV show. He said, "We need people to come and visit our recovering addicts. Addicts are being weaned off drugs and get very jumpy, so visitors would really help them and us."

"Did you hear that?" I said to Norma. I found my heart beginning to race. "He's asking for visitors."

Norma smiled sanguinely. She had got used to my enthusiasm for just about everything I got involved in.

"You're not thinking of volunteering the Messengers to go into that clinic?"

I nodded with a smile.

"But you know nothing about drug addiction," she countered in her practical way.

I laughed. "When has that ever stopped me doing anything?" I chuckled. "I think I'll give the doctor a call in the morning."

The next day I phoned the doctor and he said he'd be delighted for some of our fast-growing group to visit the clinic the following Saturday.

"Don't send anyone who is squeamish," he warned at the conclusion of our conversation.

That Saturday evening we met for prayer as usual at the Mission and then most of the team went out into the pubs and coffee bars. I handpicked a small group of half a dozen to go with me to the clinic.

It was a revelation to talk with the young men who lay on their beds chatting to our team. I saw one heroin addict roll up his sleeve and show the scars made by the needle of death. Christine, the girl talking to him, nearly passed out.

"What's the matter, luv, haven't you ever seen something like that before?" he said, enjoying the reaction he had provoked. Then he added, "I'm one of the better addicts here. I've only tried to top myself six times."

At the end of the ninety-minute visit, we went back to the

Mission to compare notes. All of us were greatly shocked to see the state of these young people.

"You know," said Norma, who had gone with us, "I wonder if God is telling us that we have to do more than just visit them in the clinic. It seems to me that it's no good if they are going in to be taken off drugs if there is no rehabilitation for them. Otherwise they just go back to them after they're released."

"Yes," I chipped in; "we need a center, somewhere we can take them and show them a living faith. But it should be outside of Birmingham, otherwise they'll be tempted to go into the city center and get more drugs."

I talked with different people, several of whom suggested I contact a local businessman. He agreed to attend a meeting at our home to discuss plans for our center. Like all of us, he was surprised when a group of addicts from the clinic also turned up to give us their suggestions.

"They're all as high as kites. Just look at them," someone remarked.

I had to agree with him. All five of the junkies who had come to "advise" us sat nodding in their chairs. It soon became evident, as we discussed the urgent situation in Birmingham, that a rehabilitation center was needed—and urgently.

Days began to turn into weeks since we had that meeting, but no real progress had been made. I was beginning to despair when one day the businessman telephoned.

"Dan, I have just read an advertisement for the sale of a place called Hill Farm in Worcestershire. Could you come and see it with me tonight?"

It took some time to locate Hill Farm, but as we drove around those narrow winding Worcestershire lanes I began to realize that the man was as excited as I was about the possibility of a center.

"That looks like it," he shouted, pointing to a farm on the right-hand side of the road. As his car bumped down the farm drive and into the courtyard it became obvious that this collection of semi-derelict buildings had been neglected for a number of years. The house was the only building that looked reasonably sound. The outbuildings looked as if they were about to collapse.

"Nine thousand pounds is the price the agent is asking," he told me, "and we need a deposit of nine hundred pounds to secure the farm." As we walked around the property, dodging the rats, the question kept going around in my mind, "Is this the place?"

On Sunday morning at the Mission, it was time for me to give out the church announcements. "If the Lord wants us to have Hill Farm, we will have to hand over the deposit within seven days," I told the congregation, none of whom had much money in the bank.

Monday morning came and I dashed to the front door. Several letters lay there and I anxiously ripped them open looking for the nine hundred pound check. All I found was a one-pound note from my Aunt Ethel in Liverpool. "Thank you, Lord," I said. "Only eight hundred and ninety-nine pounds to go."

As the week progressed, other small amounts came in that totaled about five pounds. But then, on the deadline day, I received a phone call from the businessman, saying that he wanted me to come over to his home as he had some "interesting news" for me.

His brother was there, too, and the news turned out to be that nearly three thousand pounds had been donated for the purchase of the farm.

"Dan, I think it would be right if you and Norma considered becoming the wardens of Hill Farm," he said excitedly.

"Don't forget to search him thoroughly," said the businessman as he handed over Joe, our first visitor to be cared for. Trying to look as if I searched people for drugs every day, I pointed to the bathroom and asked him if he would mind having a bath.

I noticed the blue "track-marks" on his arms made by many needles.

Joe had a cigarette lighter, which I immediately confiscated. "He's sure to try and smuggle drugs in it," I told Norma as we both peered at the lighter from every angle. Joe had, by now, finished his bath and was in the bedroom, so I slipped his "drug-smuggling tool" into my pocket and then locked myself in the bathroom. My fingers shook as I undid the midget screws that held it together. Out came the innards. No drugs in there. I peered into every corner. Still nothing. Very disappointing! Well, all I had to do was to put it back together.

One hour later, almost overcome with steam and embarrassment, I awkwardly handed back to Joe his now dismembered lighter. "Sorry about that, Joe," I said in a low voice. "It isn't quite the same, is it?" He offered me a dry smile but said nothing. Joe and I soon forged quite a friendship, though his warped obsession with death often disturbed me.

We were shoveling manure in one of the chicken sheds when he first began talking about this obsession. "I believe, Dan, that one of the most interesting forms of death is suicide," he said as he bared his snagged, yellowing teeth at me. "I've tried it five times now. Gassing. Then hanging that didn't work either. Then I slashed my wrists; and I later took a couple of overdoses."

I wiped the sweat off my face with my arm as my flesh began to crawl. "But why?" I asked as we continued shoveling and talking.

"I guess all drug addicts often have an urge to destroy themselves. They must have, or they wouldn't use killer drugs."

Our bizarre conversation was interrupted when Norma called, "Dinner's ready!" I didn't seem to have much of an appetite.

Soon the addicts were coming thick and fast from the drug clinic after undergoing treatment there to wean them off their drugs.

One of the early arrivals was David, a soft-spoken young man who seemed an unlikely junkie. He came from a pleasant middle-class home and had loving parents.

Norma perked up when she heard he was a chef.

"You could help me with the cooking," she laughed.

David was a long-time friend of Joe's and they continued their friendship on the farm. When the work periods had finished, most of the addicts would congregate in Joe's bedroom for a singsong led by Joe, who enjoyed mimicking Bob Dylan.

Each morning, after breakfast, we would have a short Bible study. While it was optional, most of the lads would stay, although often they were in violent disagreement with what I said. David rarely said much. I sometimes felt he hid his true personality beneath a veneer of politeness.

Once he did say, "Dan, since knowing you and Norma, I've changed my ideas about Christianity."

I wasn't sure whether that was a compliment or not. Then one day he came to me, his face flushed, and said, "Dan, I think I can make it now. Is it all right if I leave?" With that he smiled shyly. He had been with us a mere three months. Could he survive alone? I had my doubts.

For a while all went well; he traveled around the country, and even lived in Paris for a while. Then he came back to the Midlands. His mother bought him the equipment for a mobile disco and he visited parties around the region under the name of "Dynamite Dave."

His mother thought it would be an interest for him, to keep him off drugs. But it did not work. He went back on drugs and was readmitted to the drug clinic. While he was undergoing the treatment, he died. The shock to all of us was indescribable.

I cried when I heard the news. "Not David. Not lovable, quiet David."

His friend Joe turned to me. His face was deadly pale and his eyes were swimming with tears.

"David was my best friend," he said, his lips quivering. "If anyone deserved not to die, it was him."

But with drugs there is no discrimination.

The sheer mental torment of months of sleeping in derelict houses, and years of alcoholism and drug-addiction, was etched into Bill's pinched, emaciated features. He was in his early thirties; over six feet tall, and his unkempt fuzzy hair, droopy moustache, and wild, bloodshot eyes betrayed his years of pain and neglect.

Bill had come to Hill Farm to get off heroin.

"I want to do a cold turkey," he insisted, a look of careless abandon sweeping over his face. "Hospital treatment is too easy." A Pentecostal church in Aston, which, in turn, had contacted us for help, had helped him.

I did my customary check on Bill and was horrified to see the state of his body. There were blue scars, slash marks, track-marks and scabs.

His first night with us went surprisingly well. After a fairly good night's sleep, he spent most of the next morning wandering around the farmhouse wrapped in his scarf and overcoat.

"How are you feeling?" I would ask him periodically.

"Not bad, man. Don't worry. I'll be all right." As the hours passed and nothing happened, I began to believe that he would come through the "cold turkey" without any bad reactions.

But then Bill staggered into the kitchen where I was talking to Norma. His eyes had become as large as saucers, and a corner of his mouth was turned down and trembling.

"Dan, I can't go on. Take me to the clinic," he cried with a look of terror from deep within. "I thought I could make it, but it's no good."

I called Terry and Gary, a couple of young volunteers who were helping us, and asked them to sit with Bill as I phoned the businessman at his office.

"Can you come quickly? Bill's in a bad way," I said urgently. When I returned to the room, Terry and Gary were on their knees praying for him, while his whole body shook and his deep sobs punctured the air.

Then the businessman arrived. "Okay, Bill. Uncross your legs and sit up." He laid hands on Bill's head and prayed, "Oh, God, please help Bill at this time."

The prayer time continued for at least twenty minutes, then the breakthrough came. Bill stood up and began to smile. The pain was gone and so were the pleas to be taken to the clinic. His physical withdrawal pains had ended as quickly as they had begun.

"God's gone and done a miracle," he cried through a mist of tears.

12
Trouble Down At The Farm

Tensions were building up at the farm as petty squabbles kept breaking out among the addicts. Living in such a closed community, friction was inevitable. Bill would want the radio loud, Joe soft. I would want them to start work; they would want to laze about. Pete, a pill addict, would "fall ill" and demand I call in the doctor. Others would argue with one of our volunteers, who would accuse them of being a bunch of "ungrateful layabouts."

Norma and I were getting desperately tired with all the trouble brewing around us. Then, to make matters worse, the addicts went on strike.

"We want to do something different," Bill said brusquely. "It's like a monastery around here. We hardly get any money...." As they poured out their complaints to Norma and me, I could see my wife's face begin to flush with anger. Her working day started at 7 a.m. and often finished well past 10 p.m. Finally, she exploded and tore into them.

"You are the laziest, most ungrateful lot of layabouts I've ever met," she shouted, her voice rising to an angry tearful shout, her face stamped with harried misery. "After all we've done for you and now this is how you repay us."

The lads stood there, their mouths open.

I looked at their surprised, hurt and dazed faces. Then I joined in the verbal lashing. I turned my attention to Bill saying, "I just don't understand you."

He waited for me to finish and then responded in a voice almost too low to hear, "I'm not asking you to understand me, man. I gave up trying to do that years ago." With that he smiled bitterly.

Norma sobbed with emotion that had been building up over a period of weeks, and I took her and Andrew to the nearest bus stop so she could have a few hours with her mother in Birmingham. Gradually, the lads drifted back to work, but without enthusiasm.

Norma returned that evening and they went out of their way to stop arguing, at least for a few days.

"It was only when you and Norma flipped that we realized the strain you were both under," said Joe.

But Norma and I knew that we could not carry on forever under such tremendous pressure.

Norma's face was paper-white except for the dark circles under her eyes. She looked about as sick as a person can get. I could see from her frightened, tear-streaked face as she lay on the bed that she had been crying.

"What's up, darling?" I asked.

"Dan," she said, "I've not known how to tell you this, but I'm frightened. A lump has come on my breast." I guess we both jumped to the conclusion that this was cancer.

It was the last straw. "Lord, how many last straws are we supposed to have," I muttered under my breath wondering if this were a bad dream from which I would awaken.

Norma's visit to the doctor confirmed that an immediate operation was necessary. "We won't know if it is malignant or not until we operate," he told us grimly.

Next day, Joe and Yank, two of the addicts, headed off for a visit to the nearby town of Redditch. A member of the Hill Farm committee had given Joe permission, but not Yank.

Ten o'clock passed and still there was no sign of the pair. Joe had phoned earlier and asked if he could stay out and I had said, "no."

"Right," I said to Norma as my nerves cranked up another notch, "I'll teach them." I bolted the doors, switched off all the lights and got into bed. I felt so unhappy. Norma was ill, the addicts seemed so uncooperative, and most of the farm committee did not seem to appreciate the tremendous strain we were under.

That night, I asked Norma to read with me a passage that seemed to ask the questions that we were asking in our anguish. It was Psalm 13:1-2: How long, O Lord? Wilt thou forget me forever? How long wilt thou hide thy face from me? How long must I bear pain in my soul, and have sorrow in my heart all the day? How long shall my enemy be exalted over me?

I felt like screaming out, "Lord, why have you forgotten us? Why are so many things going wrong for us?"

We both slept fitfully that night and when I woke in the morning I went outside to see if there was any sign of the two. When they heard me coming, out of the chicken huts they came, now disheveled figures.

"Why did you lock the door?" Joe demanded. "We had to sleep with the chickens." Not a word of apology from him or Yank.

With this, something just snapped inside of me. All of the emotion that had been gradually building up just burst out. I felt I was losing the last shreds of my mind.

"I just can't go on," I said to Norma as she tried to comfort me, the tears coursing down my cheeks. "I can't handle any more of this. Let's face it, I've made a real mess of this job," I continued, as my head began to throb. She phoned the businessman and his brother and told them of my condition.

A knock came on my bedroom door. It was a deputation of addicts standing in the doorway.

"Come in, lads," I said, wiping my eyes and not really wanting to see them.

They stood by my bed and Pete suddenly blurted out, "Dan, we know you are thinking of leaving, but we want you to stay. We have just said a little prayer for you."

I burst into tears again. Norma came over to me and held my hand.

"There you are, love, God has heard your prayers. Who would have thought these rogues would have said a little prayer for you?"

They all smiled and Pete ruffled my hair as he left.

But despite that vote of confidence, Norma and I were not sure what we should do regarding our future at the farm. Whether we should stay, or go. Especially with the surgery soon to take place, Norma's health was in question.

We sought the counsel of one of the farm committee members. After hearing the whole story, he suggested we needed a rest.

"Norma smiled for the first time in a long while. I soon penned the letter of resignation. Her next smile was two days later when I left the ward of the hospital as she was about to be wheeled into the operating theater.

I locked the door of our bedroom at the farm and spent a long time on my knees. My prayer time was interrupted by the shrill of the telephone. It was the ward sister from the hospital.

"Mr. Wooding, I thought you would like to know that the operation was a complete success. The lump was not malignant!"

At last, things were beginning to go right again. Norma was soon back at Hill Farm, a little shaky, but looking rested and calm, and looking forward to the prospect that we would soon be leaving and be getting some relief from the turmoil of our time with the addicts.

The furniture van arrived at 8 a.m. on a Saturday morning. It did not take long for the movers to load our furniture and we were ready to set off.

The sad little knot of addicts came and shook hands with us.

"Thanks for everything," said Pete. "Don't feel bad about what happened. I know you're both going to make it out there."

We bumped our way up the farm drive, with little Andrew in the back seat, and moved out into a new life. Soon the new wardens of the farm came to take our place.

Norma and I spent many hours discussing why God had allowed us to go through such a traumatic experience.

"You know, Dan, I think I know why," she said one day. "I am sure God has a plan for you to one day help suffering people around the world."

I was puzzled.

"But how can a nightmare experience like the farm possibly equip me to help others who are going through trouble?"

"Don't you see? Unless you've gone through it yourself, how can you know what they are going through?

"I really believe God can't use you to care for others until you know a little about suffering yourself!"

"But I feel such a failure, love." I was feeling a great sense of self-loathing.

Norma looked compassionately at me.

"You're supposed to be the veteran Christian of the two of us, but I can tell you that Jesus also appeared to have failed when he was taken and crucified. But look what happened there. That 'failure' resulted in the greatest victory the world has ever seen. That same victory can be ours, Dan, if we just allow God to work his way in our lives. You watch. He'll turn this failure into a great victory, too!"

13
It Is Written

It was hard to summon up any enthusiasm to return to my former job filing blueprints at a large electrical company in Birmingham. I was the lowest grade clerk in that huge office, and for hour after hour I would stand by the dusty files and insert or take out blueprints for colleagues in my department.

No one would describe such work as arduous, but I came to regard it as irksome. And my feeling of melancholy was added to by the attitude of my colleagues.

"Looks like you really blew it at that drug farm," said one of them breaking into peals of insane laughter. (I've always wondered why we British enjoy others' failures more than their successes.)

"We knew you'd come crawling back," laughed another.

The swiftness with which my world had dissolved and the incomprehensible manner of its going, was a black pool into which I did not want to peer for fear of seeing my own great failure. I had gone from being the warden of Europe's first drug rehabilitation farm to the bottom of the pile in that office, and it was hard for me to take.

So, as therapy, I began making notes in my spare time about that traumatic time at Hill Farm and tried to transform these notes into a manuscript. My attempts to reconstruct the whole experience onto blank pages were painfully slow.

"You know, love," I told Norma one day, "I have noticed that Jesus and the apostles made constant reference to the written Scriptures. I read recently that "it is written" appears 106 times in the Bible. So the written word is important to God."

"What are you trying to tell me, Dan?" she asked.

"Well, I'm wondering if God is actually calling me to be a full-time writer."

Norma looked at me as if I were completely insane.

"I know you have this love for the written word, but you have no qualifications. You failed most of your exams at school, so how could you even get a job?" I paused and smiled inwardly. "Darling, my headmistress once told me that I would never succeed at anything in life if I give up at the first hurdle. Later, when I won first prize for the most improved student in the fifth year, she said, 'Go after that dream.' I plan to do just that."

My wife leaned over the table and affectionately placed her hand on mine. "Dan, do it. I'll back you all the way."

That evening, I went to the file where I kept my Hill Farm papers and I fished out a sheaf of letters from a freelance journalist, Marion Troughton. Marion had sent us a questionnaire at the farm because she wanted to write a story about our work there. I had answered her questions and she had submitted her story to me and the farm committee for clearance. For some reason, the committee had decided they didn't want the story published, so it never appeared.

I told Norma, "I wonder if I took that as a model for a story for a newspaper, if they would run it." Norma knew all about the example of Gideon in Old Testament who had put forth a fleece to find God's mind.

"Why don't you write a story and see if it gets published. If it is, you will know it is God's guidance that you should take a step further. You will then begin to discover whether God wants you to become a writer."

"But," I said anxiously, "what can I write about?"

Norma's reply was devastatingly on the mark.

"Why not the Late Night Special that you now help run at Lloyds Bank in town?"

She was right. Since leaving the farm I had reassumed the leadership of the Messengers. John Miles had done an excellent job while I was away, and the group had linked up with other outreach groups in the city including "The Ribbons of Faith." After a period of conducting this evangelistic meeting in the church hall of St. Martin's (Birmingham Parish Church) in the Bull Ring shopping center, we had taken over an old bank building in New Street and transformed it into a Sunday night coffee bar. I was chairman of the project.

The following Sunday, I persuaded a friend of mine, Dudley Thomas, to take some photographs of the meeting that was aimed at attracting people walking the streets. Then I began putting together a feature on our work.

I painstakingly typed out the words:

It is Sunday evening, the time is 9 p.m.; the place, busy New Street, in the heart of England's second city, Birmingham. A hot-dog man is doing a good trade just outside the Lloyds banking hall. He had watched the scores of young people leaving the hall in small teams. They all seemed to have red cards with "Late Night Special" printed on them. A little later they returned with many others with them.

Not exactly the material to win a journalistic award, but the only way I could test it out was to send it to a newspaper. I had a subscription to *The Christian*, a London-based weekly that had been taken over from an old-established publisher by the Billy Graham Evangelistic Association, so I decided to send it to them.

As I sent the envelope containing my story and Dudley Thomas's pictures, I asked the Lord to show me through the reaction of the paper whether I should continue any further with this apparently lunatic idea of being a writer.

I soon got my answer. The whole back page of the November 10, 1967 issue contained the photo-feature. And in the mail that day came a check for ten shillings.

I took Norma in my arms and hugged her. "If I continue in this way and get two million of these published, I could become a millionaire," I chuckled.

Her eyes were alive with excitement. "Dan, that's your answer. God wants you to be a writer."

Soon, I was devoting much of my spare time traveling the Midlands interviewing friends and sending off the results to *The Christian*. It wasn't long before my stories started appearing regularly, and I was also pressing on with the manuscript for my book, which I had given the working title of *Junkies Are People Too*.

The months slipped by, and although the articles were getting into print, I I still hadn't gotten much further in actually securing a full-time job on a paper.

"Dan," said Norma as I began to exhibit some impatience, "have patience. We know the Lord wants you to do this work. He will make it clear when you should move."

The big breakthrough came on May 16, 1968, in a letter from J. Eric Mayer, associate editor of *The Christian*. In it he commissioned me to write a feature on the relationship between blacks and whites in Birmingham's churches. Our city was fast becoming a center for immigrants from the West Indies and quite a chasm was growing between the indigenous whites and the more exuberant black population.

I jumped up and down with excitement.

"That's just what I've been waiting for," I shouted to Norma, who was dressing our son, Andrew. "They have given me a vote of confidence."

I spent nearly two weeks researching the feature, and then sent it off. Once it was published, I followed up with a letter to the editor, Dr. Jim Douglas, asking, "How about a full-time job?"

The editor was obviously taken aback by my directness, but he did agree to meet me at a writer's conference I was to attend at Hildenborough Hall in Kent. I had discovered that David Winter, a BBC broadcaster and a co-founder of the Arts Centre Group, with Cliff Richard and Nigel Goodwin, was putting on a writer's conference at this beautiful venue. I had called him and asked if I could join the group and he readily agreed.

When I arrived at Hildenborough Hall, I made a beeline for Dr. Douglas, and this shy Scot was bowled over by my enthusiasm to be a journalist. He invited me to his office in Camden Town, located in the Billy Graham London headquarters, to meet Eric Mayer.

The quiet-spoken Irishman didn't seem to mind that I did not have the academic qualifications to be a reporter.

"All I am concerned about, Dan, is can you do the job?" he asked in a no-nonsense voice.

There was an uncomfortable pause as I eyed him across the expanse of his desk, then I replied, "Well, Mr. Mayer, I think you can be the judge of that. You've seen my work and have run all of it."

He paused for a long moment and then got to his feet, leaned over his desk, and shook my hand. "Congratulations, Dan," he said in a businesslike voice. "You've got the job."

I stumbled out of the office in a happy daze. The salary they were offering was small, but even so, I was surprised at Norma's caution when I phoned her.

"Dan, that's wonderful. But don't you see that we could not live in London on a salary like that. You know we have another child on the way and that's going to make life even more difficult."

It was a job I wanted, but the reality of what Norma said struck home. Norma could not see my crestfallen expression as I struggled against the fact that the cost of living in Birmingham was low compared with London. What should we do about it?

"Norma," I said over the phone, "do you believe in that verse which says, 'My God shall supply all your needs according to his riches in Christ Jesus'?"

"Of course I do, but we have to be practical." There was a hint of sadness in her voice.

I brooded over the problem briefly, and then hit on an admirable solution. "Okay, love, then let's put the Lord to the test. If he really wants me to take this job with *The Christian*, he will have to find us a rent-free home in London."

A few days later, after a particularly tiring day filing blueprints, my father asked to see me.

"Dan, I might have some good news for you."

"Yes?" I hardly dared to breathe as I waited for him to continue.

"I've heard that there is an old gentleman in Lewisham in south London who is looking for a family to move in with him. They can live in his home rent-free if they, in return, agree to take care of him. Here's his phone number. Why don't you give him a call?"

I dialed his number and spoke with Percy Crisp, who told me he was chairman of an Eastern European mission.

"Why don't you come and see me?" he suggested. "We could then see if we would all get on."

We did, and were captivated with his large white house just off Lewisham High Street.

"We'll take it, if you'll have us," I told Mr. Crisp, an elderly man with a sharp, intelligent face and ruddy cheeks.

"I'd be delighted to have you all. I think we'll make a very happy family."

As we drove back along the M1 motorway to pack up our belongings and move to the capital city, Norma's face was alive with happiness.

"Dan," she said, "this is quite amazing. Just a few months ago we had to leave the farm. It just didn't seem to make sense." She broke into a big smile and added, "Now God has given you the one thing you've been longing for, the chance to write!"

14
I Have A Dream

My heart began to slam against the walls of my chest as I entered Shirley House, Camden Road, for my first day as a journalist. At the age of twenty-eight, I had finally gained my dream. I was more nervous than a young child just starting school, and I wasn't sure I was really skilled enough to work on a national religious newspaper.

But I threw myself into my exciting new job with great gusto.

One of my first interviews was with Coretta Scott King, the widow of murdered civil rights campaigner, Dr. Martin Luther King, Jr., who had been brutally gunned down in Tennessee just a few agonizing months before.

As I watched her four children scamper around just like any other children of their age, I thought of the pain they must all have been through.

I looked at Mrs. King and asked if she was worried about suffering the same fate as her husband.

"I have lived with the threat so long now I hardly think about it," she said her eyes ablaze. "I must do what I must do!"

She glanced across the room at her four children, and added, "My children are with me in this."

I thought of her husband's famous "I have a dream" statement. I, too, had had a dream and it had come true!

Most of my assignments were in London, so I was pleased when Eric asked me if I would go to Blackburn to interview an extraordinary patient there in a mental hospital.

"This man has written a 15,000 word book, yet he can't speak or move his body," said Eric. "In fact, he's a spastic."

As I walked into his ward, I was shocked to see the state of forty-four-year-old Bill Howe. He lay totally immobile in his bed. "How on earth could he have written a book?" I asked myself in amazement.

I began to talk with the staff and discovered that Bill had been admitted to the hospital as a "spastic imbecile." There did not seem to be much hope for Bill who was constantly ill. The medical report at that time read, "Concentration nil; unable to reply to anything; no communication."

Some of the nurses, though, were convinced that Bill was more than just a "cabbage." Christian Charge Nurse Bill Waddington took the initiative and showed him a three-penny bit and a two-shilling piece and asked him which he would choose. Through grunts and indications with his eyes, be chose the two-shilling piece. With this encouragement that there was life in Bill, Nurse Waddington, along with many others, set out to provide him with the key to a new life—education.

Amazingly, he began to learn—first numbers and then the alphabet. Bill gradually learned to speak—through his left foot! He had a large board with the letters and numbers painted on it at the end of his bed and he would tap them with his foot.

From there he learned to write by lying on his back and painting words with his foot on a stencil. This method proved to be rather slow and laborious so he eventually spelled out the request, "I would like a typewriter." The problem was, how could he possibly type? A shoe for his left foot, which was specially made, solved this and a wooden peg attached to the sole.

By this method, Bill Howe was able to write his book, *Crossed Wires*, which was published by the Spastics Society in London.

He wrote, "I found that my brain worked, but not with my limbs. It was like the wires were crossed."

This amazing author revealed what it was like to be trapped in a body for all those years without any way to communicate with the outside world. He explained how he loved classical music and how he thought the female nurses were very pretty.

When I returned to London and shared this amazing story with Norma, she said, "Dan, if it weren't for those dedicated nurses caring for Bill, he would never have learned to 'talk' through his feet. They helped a man with no voice to speak to the world."

She fixed her eyes on mine and modulated her voice and I knew that an interesting idea had just occurred to her. "Have you ever thought that as a journalist you could be used by the Lord to be a voice for those around the world who have no voice?"

She had certainly put a new thought in my mind.

A voice for the voiceless," I mused. "I wonder if it will ever happen?"

As I became more and more engrossed in my work, I began to feel uneasy about my relationship with David Coomes, the controversial features editor. He had displayed a certain amount of suspicion of me when I first started and he now seemed so aloof and distant. I made a special effort to try and win his friendship, but it was difficult. Then, one day, he confided in me that he had never wanted me to join the staff.

"But why?" I asked, startled at his bluntness.

David seemed embarrassed as he told me of his suspicion of me. "All I knew of you before you arrived was the weekly bombardment of articles you sent in," he began, his voice faltering slightly. "Some were very good, most however were not—and I was surprised the editor used so many of them. I was even more surprised when I heard that you were actually joining the paper, and thought it was an unwise step."

As he saw the hurt in my eyes, he added, "Time has proved I was wrong, and I don't mean a long time: almost at once you fitted happily into the team. You were a likeable and cheerful friend as well as a colleague, and you were soon writing much 'tougher' pieces."

By that David meant that I was sometimes critical of the events I covered. Up until *The Christian's* pioneering of "truth before PR" journalism in Britain, each rally was expected to be described as a great success.

But David changed all of that. At the time, he described his distinctive brand of Christian journalism as "honest journalism," reporting what he saw rather than what others wanted him to see. Some called it "cynical journalism," hurtful to man and degrading to God.

From the time he joined the staff in 1965 at the age of twenty-two, David tried to avoid the Christian clichés of everything being a blessing and everyone a saint. He told the truth—half-empty churches, few conversions, the ludicrous as well as the blessed, the pathetic as well as the triumphant.

Two things went wrong. Readers fastened on to his critical articles, ignoring his genuine praise for the majority of events and personalities. And they also unleashed their wrath through some hard-hitting letters.

David later admitted he did sometimes go too far, substituting personal opinion for fact, cynicism for honesty, and disillusionment for Christian love. Eventually he said that he had no defense against some readers' criticisms. "They were accurate," he said, his face stamped with pain.

Working with such a person was intimidating, to say the least. But I could see that a lot of his criticism of big-time evangelism was true. Much of British and American evangelism was like a circus.

My first insight into the problems was when I approached the leader of a certain rally afterwards for a quote.

When I told him the paper I represented, his face seemed to swell with rage. He fixed a reproachful eye on me as if I were an agent of the devil. Eventually he gave me quotes, on condition that I didn't write a critical report.

Then there was a well-known preacher who refused to shake my hand because of my connection with the paper, and some "Christian" leaders who tried to avoid talking to me.

Journalism was turning out to be quite different from what I had imagined. So, to relieve the pressure, I would work on my Hill Farm manuscript in the few spare moments I had. David had agreed to give some editorial input and I had a publisher who had agreed to take it.

Nevertheless, there was a barrier between David and me. I suppose I was something of an intruder in this strange world of *The Christian*. I knew stripping away hypocrisy was good, but needles of doubt kept pricking my conscience because I was expected to point out the failings of others, knowing only too well my own.

Our relationship changed dramatically when I was admitted to the Lewisham Hospital with viral pneumonia and was off work for several weeks. David was a constant visitor, always bringing with him books and magazines to keep me going, despite the round trip of thirty miles. He was working day and night on the editing of my book, and kept wanted to reassure me of his concern over my illness.

One day he opened up to me about his innermost feelings. "I think sometimes evangelicals fear the truth," he said laughing in a nervous, keyed-up way. "I wonder if their continued existence owes more to half-truth and sleight of hand than to the power of the Holy Spirit. I wonder if potential converts really knew what they were stepping into, whether they would ever dare to take that first faltering step into the kingdom?"

Then he began sharing about the present conflict that was causing us all so much heart-searching on the paper.

"I suppose that working on *The Christian* is showing me that there are Christians who cannot make Christianity work." His voice was edged with steel.

"I mean, it seems strange that prominent Christians should one moment preach humility, self-effacement, going the extra mile and turning the other cheek, but the next, react violently if an otherwise encouraging news report indicates that they spoke to less than a full house.

"Probably the saddest discovery I have made about some evangelicals is their inability to admit error or to apologize. Is it because by doing so they would imperil God's reputation? I believe the opposite is true. If they did these things, showing humanity and humor in their make-up, then they'd more likely enhance God's reputation as one who deals with ordinary men and not with infallible robots."

With that he left for his north London home. And I pondered this new way of thinking he had brought my way.

"Dan Wooding, this is your life." This was a special surprise for me at the Christmas party that Norma and I attended at the office after being away for six long weeks. As I was taken through my short but eventful life, I felt tears brimming at God's goodness to me. I was particularly moved when I discovered that David Coomes had been behind the presentation.

After my "life" had been well and truly presented to the assembled staff of the Billy Graham office, I was handed the "This is Your Life" book by David, and then another special package.

"This, Dan," he explained, "is your manuscript for *Junkies are People, Too*. I've finished editing it and Val Flint, the editor's secretary, has typed it up for you."

I felt the tears welling up again. This really was Christian love and concern, and from a man who was supposed to be the most infamous Christian journalist in the country. My tongue was locked.

But problems continued with the paper. David told me that

readers, unhappy with our editorial policy, were writing directly to Billy Graham to complain about us all.

I tried to push the feeling of unease away. After all, wasn't this Christmas, a time of goodwill towards all men—even journalists?

15
I Had A Nightmare

David Coomes' face was drained of all color as he put down the telephone and asked me to stop typing my story. "What's up? You look ill. Is there anything wrong?"

"Yes, Dan, there is! I've just heard that *The Christian* is going to be closed. We're all going to be laid off."

I stared at him in an almost hypnotic state. How could you close the world's oldest evangelical newspaper just like that? Surely there was a mistake.

"Jim Douglas will be calling us into his office in the next few minutes and giving us the news officially. He's absolutely shocked. He never believed the Association would go so far."

I was indignant. "I know Dr. Graham is used to asking people to get up out of their seats," I said, trying to cover my shock. "Now it looks like he's asking us to get up out of our jobs...."

I suddenly felt an overwhelming sense of bewildered desolation at a situation I could not understand.

The closure of *The Christian* was greeted with a storm of criticism from both inside and outside the evangelical community.

The London Evening News headlined the story with, "Billy Graham kills his British paper." The article began:

The 110-year-old weekly *Christian and Christianity Today* is about to be killed. The issue going to press tonight will be the last—a piece of news which the editor, Dr. J.D. Douglas, learned after his staff were told only after last week's issue had been produced.

The British Board of the Billy Graham Evangelistic Association issued a statement in the last issue of the paper expressing "reluctance and regret." They said finance was the problem, but we all suspected finance was not the only reason the paper was being axed, and only wished we had been called round a table to discuss problems with the Board.

Letters poured into the office describing the closure as "murder," and "a disaster for evangelicalism in this country," and "the heritage of more than a century's Christian journalism has been killed at a stroke."

The news became a nightmare for me. I was convinced the Lord wanted me to be a journalist and now, less than a year after fulfilling my dream, I was about to be put out on the streets.

David Coomes soon secured a position as features editor on an evening paper in Slough. In the years ahead he was to edit the Church of England newspaper, and then he joined the BBC. But how could I get a job with my lack of qualifications?

One leading journalist I called for advice said, "Dan, get out of the evangelical ghetto. There's a great need for Christians to be salt and light in the secular press. I think that's where your future lies." Then he added, "I have to warn you that it will be tough. It'll be nothing like working on a Christian paper. It can be a jungle and you may find yourself caught up in many compromising situations."

That prospect frankly scared me. I knew that working in the cocoon of an evangelical publication was relatively easy. After all, fellow believers surrounded me, and I had been told that in the secular media life was quite ruthless. I wasn't sure if I could cope with that, even if I could persuade a paper to take me on.

As I was sitting at my desk contemplating my bleak future, the phone blasted into my thoughts. It was Kevin Murphy, a long-distance swimmer whom I had asked to get in touch with me for an interview about his exploits, and about how his Christian faith had helped him in his swimming.

"Hi, Kevin," I said, trying to sound bright, but deep down feeling really depressed. "I'd love to interview you, but we've been told that we're all fired. So I have no paper to interview you for."

There was a long silence at the other end of the line as Kevin brooded over the problem. Then he told me something quite unexpected. "Did you know, Dan, that I am a journalist? I work for a newspaper group in west London that is looking for news staff. "I know that the *Middlesex County Times*, one of their papers, has a vacancy for a senior reporter right now. Why don't you give the editor, Bert Munday, a call? I'm sure he'd see you."

I called Norma at our Lewisham home and told her of the news. We had a down-the-line prayer session about it. I knew if I didn't get a job soon, I would have to return to Birmingham and face the crowing of my former colleagues who would rejoice that my dreams had, once again, come crashing down.

"Lord," Norma prayed, "we know that with Dan's lack of experience, there is no human way he could get this job. But with you nothing is impossible. So we ask you to work a miracle."

As I stood across the road from the *Middlesex County Times* in The Mall, Ealing, I became convinced there was no way I could get a position with this historic local newspaper that covered affairs in the huge, multi-racial borough of some 250,000 people. But my former school principal had told me to go after a dream, and so I had asked the Lord to again fulfill that dream even though the odds were stacked against me.

My heart was thumping wildly. "Pull yourself together," I muttered to myself. I whispered a quick prayer, and then headed across the busy road and into reception. Bert Munday, a tall man from Cornwall, with a shock of pure white hair, put me at ease immediately as I was ushered into his upstairs office by his secretary.

I handed him my business card that showed I had been chief reporter with *The Christian*. I didn't tell him, however, that I had been the only reporter, and the rest of the staff had much more important titles. He seemed impressed that he was interviewing a chief reporter, even though I knew Jim Douglas had given me the title out of the goodness of his heart.

He studied my card, and then he said, "Dan, did you know that our company printed *The Christian* each week at our Uxbridge printing plant? I used to read it as it came off the line. I thought it was an excellent paper."

Then he looked directly at me and said, "When can you start? Today?"

I was staggered.

"Tomorrow, if that's all right with you." I felt all the breath had been taken out of my body.

Mr. Munday smiled and held out his hand to me. "With your background, Dan, I think we'll start you as a senior reporter."

It was hugs all round from Norma and Percy Crisp when I brought home the good news that night.

Next morning, I was gripped by a sense of panic. And, as I walked into the office, I asked myself, "Lord, what am I doing here?" It was less than a year since I left Birmingham, and here I was working on a London paper in an area I knew nothing about. I was in over my head, and I knew it.

I was shown around the office by Mr. Munday and found the reporters friendly, but very different from my former colleagues at the Billy Graham office. Smoke curled upwards from several cigarettes, the language was different, and deadlines I was told were of "vital importance."

The news editor assumed I knew what I was doing, and immediately assigned me to interview a psychiatrist who specialized in working with drug addicts.

"Go and see what he has to say that might be newsworthy," he instructed.

I nodded blankly and drove to the address I had been given. The doctor received me warmly, and asked me which paper I represented.

I was shaking with nerves and my mind became a complete blank. "I'm from the...."

"From where?"

I looked at him desperately, perspiration rising on my upper lip, and waited for him to ask me to lie on the couch and tell him what was wrong.

"Let me take a guess," he said examining my blood-red face. "Are you from the *Middlesex County Times*?"

"That's it. You're my first interview." My nervous silence was followed by nervous laughter.

When I got back to the office I struggled over writing the story. After reading it, the news editor stormed over to my desk and exploded, "This is awful." He took a deep drag on his cigarette and snapped. "Rewrite it with a local angle and a good intro."

Whispered giggles began to break out from the other reporters in the office. A sick, sinking feeling rose up in my stomach as lazy smoke drifted up from his cigarette to form a haze.

Then he came out with a concept that I've never forgotten.

"Dan, the secret of a good news reporter is the KISS principle."

"KISS?" I asked hoarsely. I was confused.

"Yes, it means, "Keep It Simple, Stupid." Don't try and be clever in your journalism. Just write the story as it is in terms that everyone can understand."

One of the reporters took pity on me and read through what I had written. He then showed me how to re-jig it and make it more interesting.

He looked at my crestfallen expression and advised, "Dan, a good journalist should never write anything that people can't read during an average visit to the bathroom." He smiled wryly.

The next day I was assigned to interview Wilfred Brambell, the actor who played the old father in the hit British television series "Steptoe and Son." The series was exported to America in 1972 recast as "Sanford and Son."

Brambell was charming, and I remembered the name of the paper I worked for. However, I reached into my pocket and discovered, to my horror, that I had forgotten my pen.

"Mr. Brambell... do you think I could borrow your pen?"

What a disastrous start I had made with the paper. And to make it worse, I walked off with his pen!

Fortunately, with the help of the other reporters, I began to gain confidence and write stories that were accepted by the tough news editor. Then, Bert Munday decided to back his hunch that I could do the job by giving me a district to work.

"Dan, I want you to cover South Ealing," he told me. "I must warn you that it's a difficult patch. We haven't had many stories from there for ages. Just go and make friends with as many people as you can."

I did, and went from shop to shop, but no one seemed interested in giving me a story. That was, until I reached the Musical Bargain Centre, my last call of a fruitless morning.

"Hi, I'm Uncle Ernie," said an older man with a Newcastle accent who was standing behind the counter. "Would you like some coffee?" I sat down at the counter in this friendly shop which was packed full of musical instruments. Sitting at an electronic organ was a tall, blonde-haired youth, whose long fingers raced across the keyboard. He was making sounds from the organ that I had never heard before.

"Who's he?" I asked Uncle Ernie.

"Oh, a student from the Royal College of Music. His name is Rick Wakeman."

Soon Wakeman, who had long blonde hair, came over and joined us. I told him that I had recently joined the staff of the local paper and was on the lookout for stories.

"I'll give you a good one," he said brightly. "I earn some extra money playing as a session musician and I've just played piano on a track for Cat Stevens called 'Morning has Broken.' It's quite beautiful. I also played Mellotron on David Bowie's 'Space Oddity,' which I think is destined to be a number one."

I groped weakly for my notebook and jotted down what this six-foot-two-inch teenager told me.

This turned out to be the first-ever press story on Wakeman, who later went on to play with the super group YES!

Wakeman was right about the Bowie space record that in 1975, on its second release, was number one on the British charts. And "Morning has Broken" also became a hit classic around the world.

My friendship with this likeable musician grew over the months and years ahead and I eventually wrote his authorized biography, *Rick Wakeman—The Caped Crusader*, which carried a foreword by Elton John. We had many opportunities to discuss his Christian faith, and he later told me that he had been baptized and had been a Sunday School teacher at the South Harrow Baptist Church.

"Why did you get baptized?" I asked him.

"It was before I started full-time in the music business. It was like an insurance policy, a protection against the nastiness and trouble I feared could happen once I plunged into the business."

I watched in awe as Wakeman moved from being a session musician to a millionaire rock star who owned twenty-one cars, including eight Rolls Royce's. I also saw him burn himself out, the result of which was a heart attack at the age of twenty-five. It was sad to witness his marriages break up and his finances collapse. But then, Rick would pick himself up and start again.

He is now very much in business, still pushing back the frontiers of electronic rock and is now considered by many to be the world's greatest rock keyboardist for his work with YES! and also for his solo career.

"Hey, Dan, got a moment?" My news editor had the *London Evening Standard* on the line.

"Could you go over to Greenford for them? They've had a tip-off that there has been a bank robbery over there."

"Sure...."

This was my very first assignment for a Fleet Street newspaper.

Soon I was working part time for most of the big papers there, mainly covering robberies, road accidents, court and political stories in Ealing.

"What happens," the news editor explained one day, "is that each national and London evening paper appoints a correspondent to cover an area for them. They also appoint a deputy."

By this time our family had left Mr. Crisp and had moved to West Ealing, and my name was put forward as an Ealing correspondent for all the papers from the *Daily Mirror* to the *Times*.

Very soon, "Wooding of Ealing" was leading a very busy life indeed with the local paper work and the Fleet Street assignments. I was working inordinately hard to be as professional as the professionals.

Then Bert Munday called me into his office. "Dan," he said holding up the latest issue of the paper which displayed my front-page lead, "I think you're doing a fine job here. I've decided to make you chief reporter on the paper." A pleased expression flooded his face.

I tried to speak but nothing came from my mouth.

That night I took Norma out for a celebratory Chinese meal. "You know, Dan," she said as she finished her sweet-and-sour pork. "It's quite incredible what has happened to us over the past few years.

"We've run a drug farm, moved to London and seen all this happen...." Her eyes sparkled.

"Yes," I interrupted as I leaned over and kissed her on the cheek, "it's quite incredible. I've never been so happy in all my life. God has given me the real desire of my heart. I must make sure I never let him down in my work."

16
Roadblock To Moscow

Life on the *Middlesex County Times* was fascinating. There were meetings with the mayor at Eating Town Hall, overnight assignments in the parking lot of the Ealing police station where a Palestinian terrorist who had hijacked a plane was being held, and plenty of the more mundane duties of covering flower shows and sports days.

I was busy typing up the results of a school sports day at my desk when the phone rang.

"Yes," I said, leaning the receiver on my shoulder and continuing to pound my manual typewriter.

"Hi," said the voice at the other end of the line, "my name is Ray Barnett. I'm over here from Canada and I'd like to meet with you later this afternoon to discuss a proposition. I think you'll be interested in it."

This Ulster-born Canadian took me to a nearby cafe, and as soon as I ordered my cheeseburger, got down to business.

"Dan," he said as I began devouring my food, "I have been given your name as a journalist who could well be interested in something I am involved in."

I said nothing and continued eating.

He leaned over and spoke in confidential tones. "How would you like to go to Moscow for May Day?"

I stopped eating for a moment. "Are you joking?" I queried incredulously.

"I'm perfectly serious, Dan."

It was April 1973, and Ray's request seemed bizarre to me. After all, I'd never done an overseas assignment and Russia sounded dangerous.

"Look," said Ray, in his deep Ulster-Canadian accent, "I run a Christian human rights organization called Friends in the West. I understand you once worked for *The Christian*, and I thought you might like the challenge of becoming an undercover reporter in the Soviet Union."

Ray then outlined the daring plan of more than 100 young believers from eight countries who were going to attempt to demonstrate in Red Square on May Day.

"They want to call the world's attention to the Russian Christians who are suffering for Christ," he continued. "They also want to let those on the inside know there are Christians in the West who really care for them."

As we talked, I discovered that the "invade Red Square" plan had originally been announced by Brother Andrew, the Dutch-born author of *God's Smuggler* and founder of Open Doors, an organization that provides Bibles for Christians in restricted countries. But the volunteers all came from Youth With A Mission (YWAM), an astonishing movement that was founded in 1960 by an American, Loren Cunningham. The organization sends out young people for Christian service to every country of the world.

"Obviously, Red Square is going to be the place to be on May Day," said Ray. "May Day is the high holy day of communism. Brezhnev and other Soviet leaders will be there to review their troops. And the world's media will be in attendance to cover the event."

"But," I asked, scratching my head, "where do I come in? I'm a small-time reporter on a small-time local paper. Why choose me?"

"Because," his voice was now excited, "I believe God told me to approach you to undertake this assignment."

I couldn't argue with that.

Realizing he had almost hooked me, he went on. "Before you make up your mind, let me tell you more about the plan. There will be two groups going into Russia, but they will go by two different routes. The first will drive in via England in five mini-buses, the second group of fifty or so, will fly into Moscow from East Berlin.

"There both groups will meet and plan to head for Red Square and hand out copies of the *Gospel of John* taken into Russia by Open Doors. They will wear white paper crosses with slogans in Russian like, 'Christ is Risen,' 'Jesus Loves You' and 'Stop Persecuting Soviet Christians.'"

"My plan is to take in a journalist, and possibly a television newsman, to cover the demonstration from the inside," he said, watching my eyes grow wide.

"Look, Dan, we can 'accidentally-on-purpose' come across the demonstration, film and possibly photograph it, and then get out of the country as quickly as possible... if we can! You see, if the demonstrators don't get into Red Square, we can still get the story out. You and I will be right on the spot."

Ray paused for breath and then asked, "Would you like another cheeseburger, Dan?"

Norma sat silently as I outlined the proposition to her. "Isn't it risky?" she asked, wondering how she would cope if I got arrested. "After all, the Russians aren't exactly known for their tolerance of demonstrations."

"There are some dangers involved, but I guess we'll have to trust the Lord to take care of me—and the demonstrators."

Norma paused briefly and then said uncertainly, "Okay, Dan, I'll not stand in your way. If you feel you should go, I hope you enjoy your May Day in Moscow."

I suppose I was a bit melodramatic, but I wouldn't tell Bert Munday why I immediately needed to take two weeks off. However, he did allow me to place a sealed letter outlining what I was planning to do in the office safe.

"If I'm not back in two weeks, would you please pass this to Bill Molloy, the local MP. He will know what to do if I'm in prison."

"Prison?"

"I'll tell you when I get back."

Tony Tew, a BBC film editor and youth leader at St John's Church, West Ealing, which we both attended, agreed to join Ray and me on the trip. Kingsley Fewins, our navigator on the long car trip, was the fourth member of the team. He had a real concern for persecuted believers in the Soviet Union, and took care of visas and ferry tickets from England to Denmark, Sweden and Finland.

In Helsinki, we linked up with one of the teams of protesters. The fifty-one-strong group had stopped at a Christian coffee house in the city for a time of prayer and a final briefing before going "inside."

It was extremely moving to meet with these determined young Christians who had all paid their own expenses from countries like the United States, Canada, Australia, Great Britain, New Zealand and the Irish Republic to share their faith in this way.

After we had cleared all our belongings of anything that would identify us as either Christians or newsmen, Ray shouted over to us, "Okay, everyone, we're leaving for Russia now."

From Tabloid To Truth

We were leaving, he explained, one day ahead of the others. Ray turned to the YWAMers and announced, "We'll be waiting for you at the motel in Kalinin, which is about 100 miles outside of Moscow."

He then quietly added, "Don't forget, when you get there, we don't know each other. I think things will be better if we don't show any recognition."

With these words, we waved good-bye and drove off in our rented Ford Escort towards the U.S.S.R.; for some, the most fearsome land in the world.

Driving through Finland's bleak, moon-like terrain, covered with huge snow-covered rocks and grey shrubs, was an unreal experience for me. I wasn't sure whether I was scared or exhilarated by the prospect of what lay ahead. I suspect it was a combination of both.

Before we knew it, we were at the border crossing. The Iron Curtain was about to part—only a long red-and-white striped barrier barred our way.

A young Russian soldier with a cigarette drooping from his lips came to the left-hand side of the car and demanded, "Passports." Somehow his boyish looks and closely cropped hair made the situation seem less frightening.

But then Tony made a chilling observation. "Do you see that machine gun he's carrying?" he whispered.

Our tension mounted as the guard studied our faces and closely examined all of our travel documents. He eventually handed Ray, Kingsley and Tony their passports back. But, without explanation, he held on to mine, turned on his heels and strode into the guardhouse. There he picked up the telephone and held an animated conversation with someone.

"He's probably telling them you're a journalist," said Ray, his face lined with concern. "They hate journalists. They'll probably take you, and God only knows what they'll do."

"Ray...." said Kingsley, as the tension mounted in the car.

Just then the soldier came back, his face completely devoid of expression.

"This is it," I thought.

He saluted, clicked his heels, and handed me my passport. He then ushered us to proceed, manually lifting the barrier.

"Are you ever fortunate!" exclaimed Ray, with mock disappointment in his voice.

Forty suspense-filled minutes after pulling up at the border, we were in Russia. I felt a huge load had been lifted off my shoulders and said to the others, "Well, chaps, that wasn't so bad after all."

Kingsley drove gingerly along the winding forest road on the first leg of our 400-mile trip to Kalinin and then on to Moscow.

Just as I was beginning to relax I spotted them... three soldiers standing slightly back from the road under the cover of pine trees. As if on command, they sank to their knees and aimed their rifles at us. It seemed like part of a film, but it wasn't. It was real.

"What's happening?" I gasped putting my hand to my mouth. "Look, those guys are aiming at us."

Fortunately, Kingsley kept his head and didn't stop. The men relaxed, withdrew their guns, and watched us pass by.

"Welcome to Russia," said Ray, his face breaking into a huge smile. "Friendly lot, eh?"

A few hundred yards from the soldiers was a little tree. It was oddly twisted, and huddled under giant firs.

"Look," said Ray, "it's grown into the shape of a cross. It's as if the Lord is reassuring us, saying, 'Lo, I am with you always.'"

Within five minutes, we were out of the forest and had entered a completely barren area. In the distance was a menacing tower.

"This is what is known as 'death strip,'" explained Ray. "If you tried to walk across that land you would not survive. It is heavily mined and under close observation by tower guards armed with heavy-caliber machine guns."

It hadn't struck me at the time, but I had been under the impression that after the initial border crossing all the formalities would be over and we would be free to proceed. I was quite wrong.

The huge clearing we had driven into was a place of fear, guns and dogs. We pulled up to a huge customs house. A stone tower rose above the trees.

I felt my heart pound as I noticed men in blue overalls going through other cars ahead of us. Each vehicle was driven over a deep pit. A man below, armed with a thin metal rod, carefully prodded every section of the undercarriage, like a dentist searching for cavities.

Another border guard, with a periscopic device, investigated the interior of the petrol tank. The horn button was removed and examined. Door panels were removed.

"Boy, how do the Bible smugglers cope with this sort of thing?" I whispered to Tony as he sat quietly beside me.

Then snarling dogs appeared. They were put into large trucks parked alongside.

"The dogs are sniffing for people," explained Ray. "Sometimes drivers will, for a large fee, try to smuggle someone out. As you can see, it's virtually impossible."

It was then our turn to be searched and we were taken into the customs hall with our bags. Everything, including our wallets, was checked. I noticed one man was checking only for literature.

"They are especially looking for Bibles," said Ray out of earshot of the guard. "There's nothing that causes them to froth at the mouth more than the word of God. They really hate it."

After an overnight stay in beautiful Leningrad, we headed for Kalinin. The main road from Leningrad to Moscow was a potholed two-lane affair. We saw the onion-domed churches as we headed towards our destination. They looked beautiful from afar, but close up they were just shells. The front doors were locked tight and the windows were boarded up. We hardly saw one open church on the whole journey.

As we sat at the table of our Kalinin motel eating dinner the next evening with Valentine, our Intourist guide, the other fifty-one weary travelers suddenly appeared in the main dining room, and walked through into another room at the rear. They glanced at us, but showed no recognition.

What we didn't know then was that the KGB was onto their plan, and possibly ours. Some over-enthusiastic Christian in the West had released a story about the planned demonstration and a local newspaper had picked it up so the Russians were immediately alerted.

As the fifty-one Christians approached the motel, some of them had been told the trip to Moscow had been cancelled and that instead they would "tour Kalinin by special bus." The group was naturally distressed with this news and the tension mounted.

As they were finishing their main course of minute steaks, Viktor, one of the Russian guides, stood up, tapped on a glass with his spoon and asked everyone to give him their attention. His voice had a sharp uncompromising ring.

"I am about to announce our planned schedule for tomorrow," he said firmly. "We will have breakfast here in this room at 9 a.m.; take Intourist buses for the tour of the City of Kalinin, and then a boat ride on the Volga River."

With some of the girls fighting back tears, he added, "Then we will return to our motel. Thank you very much."

There was total silence in the room for a few seconds as the impact of the message hit home. Then the shock began to register on their faces.

Viktor tried to explain that there was a problem with their tour vouchers and therefore they couldn't make the planned trip to Moscow for May Day.

Our little group sat quietly listening to the band playing a mixture of Western and Russian music, when suddenly all fifty-one of the protesters stormed through the main dining room and out into the lobby. The band stopped playing while all eyes were riveted on the group as they marched past.

I heard one of the Americans shout loudly, "This is ridiculous. We didn't come all the way across Europe to see Kalinin. We are going to Moscow. I don't care what they say. Our vouchers say we can go!"

Anxious discussions were taking place all over the lobby. An Intourist official smoothed back his black hair and said to Ted (the YWAM leader), "Only those tourists with confirmed accommodation in Moscow can visit the city."

Ted retorted, "I don't believe that."

"There is no room for you in Moscow."

"Do you mean to say that in your great capital, there is no room for fifty-one people to stand on the pavements?"

Ted went on. "We are here because we love the Russian people, and we want to be at the May Day festivities. Can't you approve this?"

"We don't have the authority."

"Who does have the authority? Should we call Mr. Brezhnev or Mr. Kosygin?"

Just then a beaming Ray arrived and pulled me to one side. "Wow, Dan," he enthused, "isn't this exciting? Maybe you could start interviewing people, just in case they get arrested...."

Soon the group occupied the Intourist office. They conducted what would be considered a normal demonstration in the West.

Some were singing, "We shall overcome." I went from one little group to another taking down their names and addresses and getting comments from them about the situation.

Ted was still arguing with the officials. It took all his self-control not to completely lose his temper.

"Most of us," he said evenly, "have spent our last penny to make this trip and have gone through much hardship to get here. It would be a tragedy if we couldn't get to Moscow, the one place we have dreamed of seeing."

After about two hours, a grumpy older man stamped into the motel lobby. He looked irritated at having to leave his home late at night for such a bunch of crazy foreigners. I was called over to this man, who turned out to be the local police chief, and was introduced to him by one of the YWAMers.

"See this guy," he said pointing to me, "he's a British journalist and he's going to tell the world what has happened here tonight."

I couldn't believe my ears. Had this person taken leave of his senses? "I'm supposed to be undercover," I hissed to him out of the side of my mouth.

By this time Ted and his leaders had agreed on a plan. At 4 a.m. they were going to try to run past the sleeping guards posted at the front door and then drive off towards Moscow in their five mini-buses. But first they needed to get their passports back.

Ted asked for the umpteenth time for them and was again refused by the Intourist chief.

"Now," said Ted, knowing that a lot could take place between then and 4 a.m. At that point, the Intourist boss lost complete control and ordered them out of his office. Each member of the group demanded the right to call his embassy. Someone picked up a phone to get an outside line, but the receiver was snatched back from him.

By that time the police had also arrived and the situation looked very serious. Even so, the young people would not be sidetracked from their demands for their passports.

Finally at 1 a.m. the Intourist boss wearily said something in Russian to one of the guides standing near him. The guide, in turn, spoke, "Looks like you win. You've got your passports."

They were sternly warned not to attempt to go to Moscow, as the consequences would be "severe."

Ray took that opportunity to rescue our passports as well, but felt we should not follow on the heels of the group.

"They will definitely be picked up at the first roadblock and brought back here," he said sadly. "If we wait, we'll be able to get the whole story from them and then leave the country as quickly as possible."

Even as he spoke, a KGB conference was taking place at the motel. They were discussing how to deal with the situation.

The moment of truth came at 4 a.m. The four of us tiptoed down the stairs and hid behind pillars as the group stole down the long, wide staircase, and into the quiet lobby. As they suddenly dashed through the exit, I noticed that most of the policemen were snoring in their chairs. Not all of them were asleep, however, and as the group ran for the vans, some of the officers quickly dashed to the phone to raise the alert.

Almost in unison, keys were put into ignitions and the convoy headed in the darkness towards Moscow and trouble.

Police lights flashed and party officials in somber suits hurriedly jumped out of black sedans, and fifty-one young people milled around the car park of the Tver Motel.

All of the demonstrators were wearing white crosses around their necks with slogans in Russian like "Christ is Risen" and "Stop Persecuting Russian Christians."

Valentine, who was sitting with us at the breakfast table, shook her head in disbelief. "But," she said, "they cannot demonstrate like this in Russia. Do they not understand this?"

We all looked suitably shocked, excused ourselves, and proceeded to the lobby to talk with the demonstrators.

"Have you seen what's going on outside?" one of them asked me. "Just take a look."

I stepped outside into the freezing morning air and was greeted by a sight that chilled me to the bone. There, surrounding the motel, were about fifty uniformed figures all clutching rifles.

Gradually, we were able to piece together the story of what had happened to the group. After about eighteen miles they were faced with the impasse that Ray had predicted.

Nick Savoca, one of the group, described what happened in his book *Roadblock to Moscow*, written with Dick Schneider (Bethany Fellowship):

Far down the highway sat a giant truck-trailer parked directly across it. One lane was open but blocking it was the black sedan we had just seen. Beside the highway loomed a checkpoint tower. Even from here we could see the police van and its base and the armed figures standing around it. It was a full-fledged roadblock.

I knew it was ridiculous, but I frantically searched for escape routes leading off the highway. But the highway led us relentlessly to the roadblock.

As Ted tried to explain to the police that their visas were approved for Moscow, the situation became even tenser. For fifteen minutes the group sat there praying. Meanwhile, the police stood resolute.

Brakes squealed behind us and we looked out to see another sedan drive up. The door swung open and out stepped Andre, our old acquaintance from Kalinin.

He stood on the highway casting a long shadow behind him from the new sun. He lit a cigarette, drew on it, and exhaled the smoke as he looked at us.

Ted opened the door of his van and stepped out. I followed him along with Tony, Ralph, and a few other kids. We walked up to Andre.

He dropped his cigarette on the pavement, ground it with his heel. "I suppose by now you are very sick of me," he said wearily, "but you will not be allowed to go to Moscow."

It was by that time nearly 7 a.m., almost two hours since they had been halted at the roadblock. They were now surrounded by some thirty police and KGB men. The protesters in the vans were quietly watching the little group as they stood in confrontation with the symbols of Russian power.

Savoca looked at Ted. He could see Ted was weighing something in his mind and struggling to come to a decision.

"I knew he was praying and seeking guidance," said Savoca. "His answer wasn't long in coming."

Ted turned to the kids in the vans. "All right," he announced loud and clear. "We are not going to be allowed to go farther than here." He waited for a moment, and then continued. "I have the guidance," he stated, "that we should preach the Gospel of Jesus Christ to these people right here and now."

Savoca said an electrifying thrill shot through him. And a unanimous roar of "Praise God!" resounded from the vans. They could again openly be Christians. The group tumbled out of the vans carrying their large paper crosses. He continued:

Many held them high in the air as if they were flaming torches; others put them around their necks. And then, all fifty-one of us standing together, raised our hands to heaven, looked up and began singing lustily, "Hallelujah, for the Lord our God, the Almighty reigns....

The group stood there beside the highway and continued singing and chanting, "Christ is risen!" and "Jesus loves you!" in Russian. More police vehicles arrived and now a large number of police and security officers stood before the protesters. They were stone-faced as the group told them in Russian, "We love you... we love you."

As some snickered or stared sardonically, one policeman strode up to them as they were standing in line and singing and took close-up, head-and-shoulder pictures of each of them.

Savoca asked Andre, who had since returned to their group, "Why does your government persecute the Christians so?"

"Persecute them," he snapped, flicking away his cigarette butt. "That's what you say."

"But we have reports," said Tony, one of the group.

"False," snorted Andre, "propaganda from troublemakers."

"Then what is this?" Savoca handed him a list of names of Russian Christians now serving prison sentences for their belief. One of the group had smuggled it in under a shoe innersole.

Andre studied the list, but said nothing. Then one of the policemen took it, looked at it, and passed it to another. One pointed to a name as if he knew the prisoner.

After two hectic hours of protesting and witnessing, it became apparent that they were all under arrest. The group was completely hemmed in by police cars, vans and trucks.

Ray, Tony, Kingsley and I, all began to register our protests at being held under "house arrest" with the fifty-one YWAMers. The Intourist staff, having all got king-sized headaches by now, finally backed off and said, "Your group can leave, not the others. But you must not go to Moscow. We will give you a police escort part of the way back to make sure that you do not take the wrong road...."

We quickly told our friends that we had persuaded the Russians that we were not part of the demonstration and were off to publicize the story. They hastily gathered up film that had been taken of the roadblock protest and we did our best to conceal the film in our belongings and in the car.

After an overnight stay in Leningrad, we headed for the Finnish border. I found the situation even tenser leaving the Soviet Union than it had been going in. We thought that our film would surely be found and confiscated. The hold-up at the first border check seemed longer than before, and the guards appeared even more menacing. At the customs building, they thoroughly examined all our belongings. After about an hour of the various checks, we were told to proceed to the final border post. Even that drive wasn't without its drama.

As we headed off in the car, we heard a dreadful screeching sound under the car. Something had become lodged underneath and we were afraid sparks might cause the car to catch fire.

"Just keep going," Ray urged Kingsley. "It's a choice between possibly being sizzled alive or stopping and being shot." We just made it.

As the border guard checked our passports, Tony looked underneath the car and found a huge piece of twisted wire that had become lodged there.

As the red-and-white border pike was raised, we all offered thanks to God for getting us out safely. We also prayed for the group we had to leave behind.

Just past the Finnish checkpoint was a cafe and I began drafting the story on a napkin. Then I called the *London Evening News*, and a friend whom I had briefed about the trip put me through to one of the copy-takers. He thought I was playing a practical joke when I said, "It's Wooding of Ealing calling from Finland," for up until then, I had only done local stories.

"Are you drunk, old boy?" he asked.

"No, certainly not. I'm phoning from Finland. Look, would you please take the story."

He paused and I heard him say to a colleague, "It's Wooding of Ealing. He thinks he's phoning from Finland. I wish these guys wouldn't start drinking so early in the day."

After he finally took the story, I called the Associated Press and United Press International in Helsinki and gave it to them also. Neither one had heard a word of the incident.

"The problem," one reporter told me, "is that Moscow correspondents need two days written permission to go outside a forty-mile radius of the city." So they would not have heard about this.

The Soviet authorities finally decided to kick the fifty-one YWAMers out of the country, and a police escort accompanied them the entire 400 miles to the border.

When they arrived in Holland, Brother Andrew greeted them. He filled them in on what had happened to the other group that had flown direct to Moscow. Most of them had been confined to their hotels on May Day.

"The Russians told them they had been alerted that a group of Christian radicals were coming to stage a demonstration. Therefore, they couldn't allow anyone out of the hotel."

Brother Andrew revealed, however, that sixteen of the young people did get out of the hotel and witnessed in a park. But they were promptly arrested and expelled.

"It was obvious the Russian government had received word of your trip and were afraid," said Brother Andrew. He explained that the copies of the *Gospel of John*, which had been smuggled into Russia for them to distribute on May Day, were in good hands.

"The Russian Christians will hand them out instead," he said, "and this, too, will be very effective. I feel the Russian Christians were greatly encouraged by your outreach. Not everybody was for it. But many in the unregistered church were enthusiastic."

After such a trip, it was hard to settle back into life in the small newspaper office. Reporters that Monday morning were being dispatched to cover the local court, or to follow the mayor around on his duties.

"Dan, it's good to have you back," said the news editor. "Did you have a nice holiday? Well, anyway," he continued, "there's a really nice sports day I'd like you to pop along to cover later today. See if you can get a good human interest angle out of it...."

Welcome to Africa: *A proud dad, Alfred Wooding, holds his son "Dan Juma."*

The happy couple: *Dan and Norma on their wedding day.*

Farewell Fleet Street: *Dan's last day at the Sunday People with its editor, Geoff Pinnington.*

Uganda Holocaust: *Dan Wooding with Ray Barnett at the Nile River where thousands of Ugandans were thrown to their death to be eaten by the crocodiles.*

The Man in Black: *Johnny Cash receives a copy of "Stresspoint" from Dan Wooding in London.*

Meeting the "Saint of the Gutters:" *Dan Wooding with Mother Teresa in Calcutta in 1975.*

Marching for Freedom. Ray Barnett, broadcaster Cindy Kent and Dan Wooding at the front of the "Free the Siberian Seven" march through central London.

A New Life in a New Land: The Woodings arrive in America, 1982.

A presidential handshake: *Dan meets George and Barbara Bush in Washington, D.C.*

Meeting a great couple: *Dan chats with Billy and Ruth Graham at their home in Montreat, North Carolina.*

A case of Blind Faith: Dan with his mother as they look at the book they co-wrote together.

Still serving the Lord together: Dan and Norma Wooding, 2004.

17
From Saigon With Love

The trip to Russia caused quite a stir locally and I received several invitations to speak at different functions. After telling members of Ealing Rotary Club about the eventful trip, I was approached by a senior member.

"Dan, would you be free to go on a tour of the Far East for the London Rotary Clubs?" he asked casually. I was stunned.

"Are you joking?" I asked, feeling I had been awakened from a deep dream.

"No, I'm deadly serious. Our London district is sponsoring what is called a Group Study Exchange with our Southeast Asia region. I'd like to nominate you to go as part of our educational and cultural team."

Things moved very quickly and on a cold February day in 1974, I joined a team of young London professionals and Alan Bruce, our team leader, for two incredible months of traveling throughout that fascinating and shocking part of the world.

It didn't take long after our arrival at Calcutta's Dum Dum airport to be launched into the poverty that is India. A little boy stumped up to me swaying his tiny body from side to side. He was legless and was using his hands to propel himself forward. He could not have been more than six years of age, yet was already a seasoned (and scarred) beggar in a relentless life-and-death battle for food.

He sat upright on his stumps and held out his hand pointing to his mouth. His eyes were glazed and I thought of Peter, my six-year-old son, in England. How could I refuse him? I gave him a rupee and then, with my colleagues, set off in a taxi into the festering, foundering metropolis where hundreds of thousands of sick, starving human beings lived a lingering death in the gutter.

The sights I encountered in Calcutta will remain with me for the rest of my life. Cows were everywhere. They were asleep on the sidewalks and in the roads, possibly reflecting on the good fortune of being sacred in a world where Philistines everywhere else ate their unfortunate relatives.

In the city, my heart went out to the barefoot children who trailed after us asking for money and not accepting "no" for an answer. They padded along, touching my arm and pointing to their mouths. Whole families lay on filthy sidewalks outside decaying buildings that once housed the British. Babies suckled vainly at dry breasts after being born in the dust days before.

Our team stood stunned as we watched Mother Teresa's Sisters of Charity fought to stem the advancing tide of disease and hunger. They doled out soup and bread to the endless line of starving people at one center. We saw one of their trucks setting off with a cargo of food, for a leper colony.

We toured a home for abandoned children and saw cots containing tiny helpless babies found in gutters, alleyways, or simply handed in by desperate mothers who couldn't cope with yet another mouth to feed.

As I tried to comprehend the misery, I wondered how such a situation could be allowed to exist.

"Why do you do this work?" I asked one of Mother Theresa's nuns, who came from Ireland.

"We do it for God. We are told in the Bible that if we even give a cup of cold water to one of his children, we are doing it for him."

These selfless people were a great challenge to my faith as a Christian. I had never seen such life and death situations before.

Little did I realize that the following year, I would meet Mother Teresa personally and have the opportunity to interview her.

Mother Teresa of Calcutta was small in stature -- she stood only 4-foot-11-inches tall—but she was a giant to the have-nots of life that she ministered to during her six decades on the subcontinent of India, as well as others around the world. Her friends were the starving, the dying, the poor.

When I visited her at her headquarters in Calcutta back in 1975, I immediately warmed to this gentle, Yugoslav-born woman, who went on to win the Nobel Peace Prize, for she had seen more poverty than anyone I had ever met. Speaking in the founding, festering slum where she made her simple home, I was surprised to hear her express pity for the "poverty-stricken West."

"The spiritual poverty of the Western World is much greater than the physical poverty of our people," she told me, as the fan whirred above us, trying to alleviate the unbearable heat of the Indian city.

"You, in the West, have millions of people who suffer such terrible loneliness and emptiness. They feel unloved and unwanted. These people are not hungry in the physical sense, but they are in another way. They know they need something more than money, yet they don't know what it is.

"What they are missing, really, is a living relationship with God."

Mother Teresa cited the case of a woman who died alone in her home in Australia. Her body lay for weeks before being found. The cats were actually eating her flesh when the body was discovered. "To me, any country which allows a thing like that to happen is the poorest. And people who allow that are committing pure murder. "Our poor people would never allow it."

And the teeming millions of the poor of the Third World have a lesson to teach us in the affluent West, Mother Teresa declared.

"They can teach us contentment," she said, her leathery face gently smiling. "That is something you don't have much of in the West.

"I'll give you an example of what happened to me recently. I went out with my sisters in Calcutta to seek out the sick and dying.

"We picked up about 40 people that day. One woman, covered in a dirty cloth, was very ill and I could see it. So I just held her thin hand and tried to comfort her. She smiled weakly at me and said, 'Thank you.' Then she died. "She was more concerned to give to me than to receive from me. I put myself in her place and I thought what I would have done. I am sure I would have said, 'I am dying, I am hungry, call a doctor, call a Father, call somebody.' But what she did was so beautiful. I have never seen a smile like that. It was just perfect. It was just a heavenly gift. That woman was more concerned with me than I was with her."

Mother Teresa, who had a wonderful way of making you feel you were the most important person in the world when you were talking to her, told me of another incident.

"I gave another poor woman living on the streets a bowl of rice," she said. "The woman was obviously starving and she looked in wonder as I handed it to her. "She told me, 'It is so long since I have eaten.'

"About one hour later, she died. But she did not say, 'Why hasn't God given me food to eat, and why has my life been so bad?'

115

"The torture of hunger and pain just finished her, but she didn't blame anybody for it. This is the greatness of our poor people."

Mother Teresa added: "We owe a great debt of gratitude to those who are suffering so beautifully. They teach us so much."

When I flushed as I asked Mother Teresa her age at that time, she told me: "There is no need to be embarrassed. I'm 64."

She added with a twinkle in her eye: "I'm getting old now aren't I? But it's a wonderful thing to be able to spend all those years for God."

When I met her, she was still not well know. But she went on to be called "The Saint of the Gutters" and died on Friday, September 5, 1997 surrounded by grieving sisters of her order. She was 87.

After a short spell in India, we moved on to Singapore where we addressed several Rotary Clubs and were shown around this city-state that has one of the highest standards of living in the Far East.

From Singapore we went to Malaysia and then across to Sarawak, Sabah, and Brunei in Borneo. We arrived in Bangkok, Thailand, where the Bangkok Post called us the "emissaries of goodwill."

There came a possibility of finishing our tour in South Vietnam but, not surprisingly, I found that the rest of the team didn't feel too happy about going on to Saigon, so I made the decision to go there on my own.

"A Dr. Wang will meet you at the airport," I was told by our leader, Alan Bruce. "He is a leading Rotarian in Saigon."

I don't think I had ever prayed so much as, when our plane flew over Vietnam. As I looked down, I felt terror as I saw hundreds of bomb craters pock-marking the whole countryside. This indeed was a country scarred by a terrible war.

At the time, Americans had withdrawn their 500,000-strong army and, despite the so-called peace agreement with Ho Chi Min, the Viet Cong were continuing their inevitable push towards Saigon.

"I am surprised a journalist would come here now," said the passport control officer at the heavily guarded Saigon International

Airport. "We are facing a nightmare, yet the world's press largely ignores our plight."

He smiled as he handed my passport back to me. "Have a good stay in my country," he said, adding, "And write the truth!"

I thanked him and headed out through the barrier. I looked in vain for the doctor, but he was not there. My heart was now pounding violently. What should I do? I was in a strange and dangerous country. And all I had with me was a piece of paper with his name and phone number on it.

A kindly airline employee agreed to call him and discovered he was dealing with patients. Apparently he had been given the wrong flight to meet, and had returned to his surgery thinking that I had decided not to come after all.

"He wants you to take a taxi to this address," she told me.

After passing through the various airport roadblocks, we were soon tangled up in a mess of bicycles and mopeds that were clogging up the road. There were also many horse-drawn carts, now back in favor in this war-torn land. We passed two men who were fighting at the side of the road. It was a violent scrap with fists and feet being used equally.

"You Yankee?" asked the driver.

"No, I'm English," I responded.

His face lit up. "I'm glad. Yankees gone and ditched us. They said they were our friends, then they left."

His face became very serious.

"You tell the people in your country that we will fight to the death. But still the VC will win."

Soon we pulled up outside a large house surrounded by a high wall. The driver honked his horn and a girl opened the gate and let us in.

"Is Dr. Wang in?" I asked.

She bowed.

"He's at work. But wife is here."

As I went into the house, Mrs. Wang, a slight Chinese lady, greeted me.

"You are welcome in our home. Thank you for coming. Not many people do these days."

After Chinese tea and polite conversation, Dr Wang arrived.

"Mr. Wooding, I can't thank you enough for coming to Saigon.

You will get a deep insight into the real truth about what is happening here."

As the courses of the Chinese meal were served to us, the stocky doctor told me his story.

"My wife and I came here from Shanghai about twenty-five years ago when I was a newly-qualified doctor. I was really shocked when I saw the plight of the thousands of poor people living here. So we both decided to settle. Since then I have treated more than a million Vietnamese free of charge."

I gasped.

"Do you know that in our war-torn land we now have about 400,000 war orphans?"

When I was shown to my bedroom on the second floor, Dr. Wang informed me that the room had been taken over by the Army during the Tet Offensive, when the Viet Cong had tried to take over Saigon.

"There were gun battles going on from your balcony," he said in a matter-of-fact way.

Having never been in a war zone before, I was finding the tension difficult to cope with.

The next morning I wanted to take some photographs of Dr. Wang's Rotary Clinic for children, which was across the road from his home. As I pointed my camera and pushed the shutter, an arm came around my neck and began throttling me.

"Argh...." I made a sharp glottal sound of surprise. I could feel myself losing consciousness as I fell backwards.

Then I heard Dr Wang's angry voice shouting at my assailant.

"Let him go," he yelled loudly, his eyes bulging with fury. "He's with me."

The man eventually let go of my throat and I got up from the ground and looked up at a young man with a terrible scar across his face.

"I am sorry for that Mr. Wooding," said the doctor. "He thought you were photographing the machine-gun post in front of the clinic. Men who have been injured in battle, like this one, are stationed to watch for suspicious characters that try and photograph military installations. If I were you, I'd be a bit more careful with that camera."

As I sat with him during his surgery and saw the never-ending stream of youngsters, he turned to me and said, "My philosophy is simple. To safeguard children is to safeguard humanity."

After I spoke at the Saigon Rotary Club, Dr. Wang arranged for me to visit a refugee camp well outside of Saigon. It took a special pass to get there through the various roadblocks and a driver and a guide were arranged for me.

When we arrived at the Camp—a few corrugated iron huts on a desolate piece of ground—I was taken to the main gate where a couple of soldiers were jabbering away in Vietnamese on walkie-talkie radios. They examined my documents and then ordered me to follow them. Suddenly I was being held in a hut and the men were now shouting at each other in an excited way.

I looked desperately to my guide for an explanation.

"They think you are a Viet Cong spy." A jittery smile hung on her face.

I uttered a shaky little laugh.

"I don't know," I thought to myself. "The Russians detained me and now these people think I'm on the opposite side. The world's absolutely crazy."

The guide was deeply embarrassed.

"It seems that your papers are not completely in order and everyone is very jumpy these days about the VC."

Eventually, I was ordered at rifle-point to reboard the mini-bus to Saigon.

"Mr. Wooding," she said gently, "you will be pleased that they now say they believe you are not a spy, but you cannot look around the camp until you get the proper documentation."

Next day, I was able to get the right paper and went back, this time to be treated as a VIP. I was able to interview whomever I wished and to take as many photographs as I wanted.

Each day in Saigon, I met heroes. Relief workers, medical staff, and missionaries—all of whom would not leave their posts of duty.

"We know we could be killed, but we will not leave," said one American missionary. "God has called me to Vietnam and here I will stay—until the very end."

When the time came for me to leave Saigon, I had tears in my eyes. I thanked the doctor and his wife for their kindness to me during my stay.

"My eyes have been opened by this visit," I told them. "Any

time you are in England, I would be honored if you would come and stay with Norma and me."

The couple did stay with us for a time in our new home in Walton-on-Thames and became valued members of our family.

Dr. Wang and his wife looked as if they had been through a nightmare when they arrived at Heathrow Airport. It was just one year since I had been with them, and Vietnam had fallen to the Communists. The couple, who had dedicated a quarter of a century to serving the people there, had been forced to flee for their lives. The country was in turmoil.

"We lost almost everything," said Dr. Wang after I introduced him to my wife. "We are going to have to start our lives again from the beginning."

I discovered that some of Dr. Wang's former patients were in England at the Ockenden Venture Home in Haslemere. The orphans had been flown over to England by a newspaper that had mounted a last-ditch effort to rescue the children from the mayhem that was expected to result from the fall of Saigon.

The paper had prominently featured the airlift, but had come in for considerable criticism for taking the children out of their natural environment, however bad it had been. But I was still shocked with the apparent callousness of the man on the picture desk when I told him of this reunion between Dr. Wang and their "war orphans." "We've gone off Vietnamese war orphans, old boy," he said curtly. "Sorry, we're not interested."

"But you brought them over...."

With that the phone went dead.

The doctor and his wife have now started their lives again in another part of the world, and when I saw them off at Heathrow Airport, I suddenly felt ashamed of part of my profession. The words of that man on the picture desk kept replaying in my mind.

"We've gone off Vietnamese war orphans, old boy."

Then I thought of the words of Jesus: "As much as you do it unto these children, you do it unto me."

18
A Tale Of Two Prisons

My phone rang at the *Middlesex County Times*. On the line was the cultured voice of a local clergyman who had allowed me to do a story of his friendship with Britain's most notorious gangsters, the Kray brothers— Ronald, Reggie and Charlie—who were all currently in prison for their misdeeds.

"Dan, I've just had a call from Violet, the boys' mother," he said in his rich accent. "She likes your article and wants to invite you for tea."

I was dumbfounded. "But, isn't that dangerous?"

"No, not at all," he said confidently. "She's a lovely lady. Don't believe all you read in the papers." I heard him chuckle on the other end of the line.

Sitting in the small office with me was Mike Watson, the copy editor. He could see the color had drained from my face. "What's up, Dan?" he asked. "You look as if you've had a nasty shock."

"I have," I said quietly. "Violet Kray has asked me round for tea! Do you want to join me? I think I need some moral support."

I had read so much about this family; how they were said to have controlled London's underworld and were blamed for many shocking acts. So tea with the matriarch of the Kray family, whose name was synonymous with violence, was an intriguing and frightening prospect.

My heart was pounding unmercifully as Violet, an open-faced strawberry blonde, opened the door of their London flat and welcomed us inside. Both she and her husband, Charles, a small, thin-faced man, made Mike and me feel at home in the place where the police had arrested twins Ronald and Reggie.

Their living room was comfortable, and all over it was evidence of the boys' regard and affection for their mother. Hanging on one wall was a painting of a cottage surrounded by green fields. It was Ronnie's first painting with oils. His studio was a cell in Her Majesty's Prison, Parkhurst, on the Isle of Wight. On another wall was a British Amateur Weightlifting Association certificate presented to Reg for his weighty exploits in the prison. Dotted around the room were also brightly colored, beautifully made teddy bears and other soft toys. Ronnie and Reggie had made them as presents for their mother.

There was a haunting sadness in Violet Kray's eyes when she said in a barely audible voice, "I can't tell you how much I miss the boys. They were everything to me."

Then she locked her confused eyes on mine. "Dan, I enjoyed reading your story in the Ealing paper. Ronnie has read it and I have a little note for you from him."

It was handwritten on toilet paper and on it Kray "suggested" that I should write a book called "Kray Country" which was to be for "propaganda purposes." It would, he said, be full of quotations and stories "from celebrities who have met us and know us well". There followed a list of top British show business and political personalities that read like a "Who's Who." I could hardly believe that this man, whom some had called Britain's Al Capone, was giving me a "request" I could hardly refuse.

I looked desperately at Mike for moral support. He appeared to be embarrassed too. After another cup of tea, we left. Violet saw us into the graffiti-marked elevator, and I heaved a sigh of relief as the doors squeaked close.

"Well," I said to my companion as we headed for the ground floor, "there's a turn-up for you. How am I going to get out of this one?"

Mike smiled faintly and said nothing.

Then came an invitation from Reggie Kray for me to visit him and his twin brother in Parkhurst. I also received a letter from the Prison Governor saying that if I wished to be placed on the approved list of visitors I would need to fill in the form that was enclosed and also send two passport-type photographs. Shortly thereafter a police officer appeared at my home to "check me out."

When he discovered that I was a journalist and that I hadn't known the twins before their imprisonment, he told me he didn't hold out much hope that I would be allowed to visit Reggie.

He was right! I received a letter from the Governor saying that he had received instructions from the Home Office "to the effect the regulations do not permit your name to be included as an approved visitor or correspondent to 058111 Kray."

A huge relief flooded over me. I was frankly quite scared to visit this infamous pair, but still Violet kept in contact and urged me not to give up on the book project. I mentioned the idea to a Fleet Street contact on the *Sunday People* and he suggested that they could be interested in a special series on the life of the Krays behind bars.

Although I was not an "approved correspondent" with the Krays, I began writing to them regularly and receiving their replies. It was fascinating to be conducting correspondence with these two men who wrote to me as if I were an old friend. The authorities never stopped any of the letters, so I just kept writing.

The newspaper was, by now, pressing for as much material as I could muster, and so I began to write out lists of questions for the twins, and Violet would smuggle them into Parkhurst for me. The following week she would bring out the hand-written replies, usually from Reggie.

He wrote on one occasion from his cell in the Maximum Security block:

> It's a sanctuary for me, just like one's own bedroom outside. That's why I don't like other people in my cell. It's cozy with a writing desk, a toilet stand, two other tables as well, with my record player and radio on them. There's a photo of Mum on my desk, a photo of my girl Christine on the other table, and one of Frances, my late wife, and myself, on the wall. The bed has a flowered cover on it.
>
> There's a calendar on the wall, sent by a friend with these words which seem appropriate for one in my predicament:
>
> > Oh Lord, grant me the serenity to accept
> > the things I cannot change;
> > The courage to change the things I can
> > And the wisdom to know the difference.

Through Violet I was able to send in Christian books, a copy of the *Living Bible* and many Christian records, all of which were gratefully received by the twins.

As I began to research the feature, I was introduced to many friends of the Krays. One day Violet let me drive her around the ugly streets of London's East End, where the family had lived for most of their lives. Many of the terraced houses there had been demolished and were replaced by groups of grotesque high-rise concrete cellblocks. It was Moscow come alive in the city where Karl Marx toiled for years creating Communism with pen and ink.

I noticed the pub that looms large in Kray folklore, the "Blind Beggar," where Ronnie is said to have coldly shot gangster George Cornell, a member of the rival Richardson gang, and then walked out, banking that the East End would not talk. But it did!

"Turn left past the Blind Beggar and that will bring you into Vallance Road where we used to live," Violet told me.

For a few brief moments I was taken back a generation as we toured the little cobbled back streets of Bethnal Green. As my car moved at walking pace, the motor whining in first gear, I saw the pub where Violet used to be a regular, the corner shops where she and the boys shopped, the park where the twins played as children and the cafe they used as the headquarters for their early villainy. The "two-up two-down" terraced houses no longer stand there, having been replaced by a few corrugated iron fences hiding a future building site.

As I stopped my car, she pointed to the spot where police cars would park twenty-four hours a day.

"They used to sit there watching who went in and out of our house," she said with a face white and strained. "Ronnie would feel sorry for them and one night said to me, 'Mum, I think they must be hungry and thirsty sitting out there in the cold. Do us a tray of tea and biscuits and I'll take it out to them.'"

"They were most grateful. One of them brought it back a little later and thanked Ronnie very much."

But now, because of their crimes, they had, in Orwell's parlance, become "un-persons."

Soon I was to meet one of the Kray brothers. The eldest, Charlie, was to be allowed out of prison for a spell of acclimatization before possibly being freed. He was not thought to have played such a serious role in the crimes attributed to the twins.

The Sunday People asked me if I would try and gatecrash his welcome home party, but that wasn't necessary. I phoned Violet, and she said I could come as a special guest.

One day Ronnie wrote and said he had been delighted to read of a kind remark about the twins in a book, *For Adults Only*, by Diana Dors. I phoned Diana with the news and she suggested that I take her and her husband Alan Lake over to see Violet, her husband Charles, and Charlie, who had been released from prison. With a delicious sense of voyeurism I watched the discussions unfold as many fascinating stories were relived.

When the articles appeared under my by-line in *The Sunday People*, several members of the Kray family and their friends made it clear to me in no uncertain way that they were not pleased with some of the material. For a time I became very concerned for the safety of my family and myself. After all, you didn't mess with the Krays. Fortunately, nothing happened to us.

I felt a flush of sheer excitement as I stepped off the Ethiopian Airlines plane at Lagos Airport and into the sauna-like heat of West Africa in the summer of 1976. At last I was back in Nigeria, the country of my birth. I had been in Kenya for an American relief agency and they had asked me to go on to Nigeria to cover another aspect of their work.

"I'm here to discover my roots," I grinned to the Englishman who waited in line with me for the immigration officer to check our passports. "I've always wanted to return here."

My traveling companion presented his passport and was waved through.

"See you on the other side," he mouthed as he disappeared into customs.

I smiled warmly at the official as he began studying my travel document.

"Where's your visa?" he snapped in a most unfriendly fashion.

"Visa?" I asked. "Why do I need a visa? I was born here."

"Are you a Nigerian citizen?" he asked in rapid-fire fashion, his eyes throwing off sparks.

"No, but...." My cheeks turned to bright crimson.

"You will pick up your baggage and follow me."

In a state of shock, I staggered under the weight of my baggage, struggling to keep up with the striding official as we wove our way through the crowds milling about. Obviously, I thought, we were going to have a cup of tea and rationally discuss this problem.

He stopped suddenly outside a door marked "Detention Cell." He unlocked the door and said, "You will stay in there until we decide what to do with you." With that, he got behind me and gave me an unceremonious push into the cell that already held four African prisoners. I stood there frozen with shock for a moment, not totally comprehending what was happening to me. It had all taken place so quickly that I had had no time to react.

Then I noticed that one of the Africans was on his knees on a straw mat praying towards Mecca. He stopped suddenly and gazed at me in shocked disbelief. The others stopped their babble of conversation and sat staring at me.

"Err... I'm Dan Wooding from England," I stammered. Then, as a reflex action, I reached into my top pocket and brought out my business cards and handed one to each of them.

The Africans looked at them in bewilderment and gathered around me. "What have you done?" asked one.

"I don't know. I think it's because I haven't got a visa."

Two of them explained they were from Senegal, the others from Mali. They told me they had also arrived without visas.

"We are starving. They have given us no food or for two days," said the man who had by now given up praying to Allah. "I'm trying to sell my sewing machine pay for my fare out." He faced me square on. "Would you like to buy it? It's a Singer, you know."

I looked at the sturdy, black machine with its famous trademark and tried to explain that I hadn't much use for a sewing machine at that very moment.

In blind frustration, I began banging on the door demanding to be allowed to speak to the British Embassy in Lagos. There was no reply, so I angrily wrote a note that read, "I demand to know why I am being treated like a dog," and slipped it under the door of the cell.

A guard quickly picked it up. He read it and shouted, "Shut up, white man, otherwise you'll be in even more trouble."

I suddenly felt a growing terror, as I knew that this was no idle threat. I had read the press stories of executions being carried out on Nigerian beaches and soccer stadiums, and being transmitted live on television. My flesh began to crawl as I realized the serious situation I was in.

I noticed there were only four bunk beds in the cell and there were five of us. One of the Africans read my mind and pointed to the bed he had been lying on.

"Take it," he said kindly as he fingered his prayer beads. "I will sleep with my brother."

It was now dark outside and the stark, bare light bulb that glared from the ceiling cast strange shadows around the room. In the office next door I could hear the guards shouting and laughing. They were speaking in the Hausa language, so I couldn't understand what they were saying, but that made their echoing conversation seem even more ominous to me.

The heat in that tiny room was stifling and my throat tightened. "I began to shake with a combination of fever and fear, not knowing what was going to happen to me. I tossed and turned on my bed as beads of sweat covered not only my face but also my entire body. I felt closer to death than I had ever done and began to realize how helpless prisoners must feel when the cell-door is locked and they are locked up for hours at end. Mosquitoes buzzed around my face, and as I continually swatted at them I wanted to scream with frustration.

1 looked through the meager light from a single bulb at my fellow prisoners. They were of a different faith, yet appeared to be taking the situation much better than I. I felt a great shame at that moment.

I managed to find my Bible in my suitcase and asked them if they would mind if I read it. "You see," I explained, "I'm a Christian so we're all people of "the book."

They nodded. I fluttered the pages of my Bible and found myself reading passages from Matthew and finally my eyes settled on chapter 25:36, "I was sick and you looked after me, I was in prison and you came to visit me."

"Lord," I prayed silently, "I really need you to visit me this time. I'm scared, really scared." I felt a choking sensation in the base of my throat, and the sharp sting of tears.

All of a sudden the fear melted away and I felt an all-enveloping peace come over my whole body. I continued to leaf through my Bible and came to Hebrews 13:3, a verse I had never read before: "Remember those in prison as if you were their fellow prisoners, and those who are mistreated as if you yourselves were suffering."

I began to pray again. "Lord, are you allowing me to experience what it's like to be in prison so that I understand? I know I'm here because I did something stupid, but there are many in countries like Russia and China who are in prison just because of their faith."

I began to try and imagine what it must be like to be incarcerated in the Soviet Gulag for twenty years or in a Cuban prison on

Castro's Caribbean island. The prospect was unthinkable, yet a living nightmare for hundreds, maybe thousands, of my brothers and sisters around the cruel world of ours.

As I gasped for air in that dank cell I could hear the others quietly chanting Koran verses to a backdrop of buzzing mosquitoes. I was finally able to sink into a fitful sleep and awoke some hours later, parched and with a terrible headache. I felt feverish and my face had swelled to terrible proportions.

Finally, the cell door was unlocked and a guard shouted to me, "Hey, you will come next door and speak with the chief immigration officer. But leave your shoes off. We don't want you to try and escape." He eyes had become ugly slits and I heard a metallic click from his rifle.

The official was equally unsympathetic.

"You can protest all you like, Mr. Wooding, but are still going to be kicked out of the country," he said with an indifference that chilled me. "You have arrived without a visa and you cannot enter Nigeria." His voice dripped with contempt.

"Can I say something, please?"

He yawned, stretched and nodded as he eased his well-polished boots up onto his well-littered desk.

"I came here with nothing but goodwill for the country of my birth. Now you make me feel ashamed to have those feelings. You are doing all you can to make me hate Nigeria. But that is not going to happen. Jesus told me to love everybody and I'm going to love you all."

I tried to continue, but he cut in, his eyes bulging from behind his steel-rimmed glasses. "Okay, enough of the speech," he said abrasively. "We are arranging for you to take a flight to London this morning. You can have breakfast here at the airport, but you'll have to pay for it."

With my shoes returned to me, I was frog-marched at gun-point to the restaurant where I was able to order bacon and eggs. They had never tasted so good! My guard watched my every move with an expression that was both amused and contemptuous.

Back in the cell, I said goodbye to my new-found African friends, and not long afterwards I was told that it was time to leave. I was roughly bundled aboard the plane, and was not allowed to have my passport back until we were in the air.

Norma was shocked when I appeared at our front door and told her what had happened to me. Her voice was soft as she said, "Don't think it was all a waste of time, Dan. I know the Lord allowed you to experience the prison cell to know what it's like to be locked up. Maybe one day he's going to have you write about people who are imprisoned."

She paused for a moment, and then added, "I know it wasn't pleasant for you. But I also know that God doesn't allow anything to happen to us without a reason. One day that reason will become completely clear to you."

19
"Who And What Is Dan Wooding?"

After four years of stringing, I was offered a job on the *Sunday People's* reporting team. It wasn't long before I was in the middle of the fray with the other news hounds of Fleet Street, chasing after the big exclusive stories.

I worked in this frenetic atmosphere for three years. It was exciting in the beginning with but eventually it began to feel like I was working in a cesspool, as many of the stories were so destructive and depressing.

Among the stories I wrote about were Diana Dors' "love affair" with Elvis Presley; the life of Melody Bugner with her boxing champ husband; and the heart-attack story of Eric Morecambe, the comic from the Morecambe and Wise duo; plus a host of stories with personalities like "Carry On" actress, Barbara Windsor and comedian, Larry Grayson. All these people were very popular in Britain at the time.

It was while I was interviewing Eric Morecambe about his illness that my frustrations with my life in Fleet Street began to come to the surface. After listening to his story at his home, I told him that I was having real problems as a Christian coping with some of the ethical problems that faced me.

"Eric, I don't know if my conscience will allow me to stay in Fleet Street much longer," I told him. "I think I'm going to have to get out."

The comedian looked at me very seriously. "Dan, you are very fortunate to be able to afford a conscience. Most people in this world can't afford to have one! Most people in Britain do what they have to do to survive."

I was shocked by what he said. Morecambe was saying that most people just have to survive—whatever it takes. Was that the way Christians should live? Should we just join the rat race or should we opt out? What was the answer?

Besides the struggles I was having with my conscience, Norma was also concerned with my drinking habits, which usually took place in the smoke-filled Stab in the Back, the pub in New Fetter Lane, just off Fleet Street, then the Mecca for the British newspaper scene.

I justified my large intake of German lager by telling myself that I was just doing the same as my fellow scribes. The booze helped to blunt the pain I felt in dealing with so much human anguish. Because of the type of paper I worked on, we attracted the bizarre and the tragic. It seemed as if I spent most of my time grubbing around the garbage cans of British life. Instead of writing something worthwhile, I felt I was just helping to present a freak show of stories for an audience that craved sensation, not beauty.

It all came to a head one evening when I heard the words "I'm going to kill you!" issued by a Scotsman whose insane eyes scanned my face, He drew deeply on his cigarette and slowly blew the smoke out, watching as it snaked upwards towards the grubby ceiling of The Stab in the Back.

I smiled weakly as I stood at the side of the bar and stammered, "But why? What have I done to you?"

The Scotsman gulped a double whisky, turned to me and hissed, "Because you know where Maurice O'Mahoney is and he put one of my friends behind bars."

The O'Mahoney he was referring to was a London criminal mastermind turned informer. A criminal by the age of ten, he had been involved in nearly every type of crime known to man, from hijacking trucks and bank raids to highly professional burglaries and wage snatches. But when O'Mahoney was caught, he informed on more than 200 criminals involved in crimes totaling over one and a half million pounds (about US$ 1 million at the time.)

Now O'Mahoney was facing life on the run. An underworld contract was out on his life and he lived in constant fear of being tracked down and savagely killed.

I had co-authored a book called *King Squealer* with this criminal who always carried a Magnum whenever we met at a series of secret hideouts. The story was serialized in the *Sunday People*.

As I tried to stop my whole body from shaking with fear, the hit man continued, "There is only one thing that can prevent you from dying tonight... you have to tell me where that swine is. If you don't, well I've got a knife in my car outside and I plan to get it and slit your throat."

My mind raced for a response as his huge, staring eyes bored into my very soul. I knew he was not joking as his reputation had gone before him. My brow was awash with perspiration as he ordered another Scotch from "Boy George," the large, curly-haired bartender who so enjoyed "mothering" the many journalists that packed the pub.

"But," I responded, as a lump gnawed at my throat, "I... don't know where O'Mahoney lives. He never told me where I could contact him... just in case of a situation like this."

I tried to catch the eye of another reporter hovering nearby, but he was intent on his conversation with a reporter from the *Daily Mirror*. I desperately scanned the bar, hoping that someone would help me. Suddenly, one of my colleagues, seeing the look of terror on my face, ambled over.

The Scotsman was not pleased and blew smoke into his face. "Hey, there's no need to do that," my fellow scribe protested as he wiped the stinging smoke out of his eyes. "Anyway, what have you been saying to Dan?"

Before he could answer, I responded, "He says he will kill me unless I tell him where O'Mahoney is." With that I heaved myself onto a bar stool and hooked my legs around it.

"Look," he said, eyeing my potential killer, "I don't know what your game is, but don't come in here making threats like that. Dan is just doing his job. If you want to get your revenge on the "squealer," that's your business. But don't go behaving like this."

I could see two heads "rolling" by the end of the evening, if he continued.

The arguments about whether or not I should die continued for an hour amid the smoky swirl of the executioner's omnipresent cigarette. Drinks were bought and downed and gradually the atmosphere brightened a little.

As he swallowed another double whisky, I ventured, "I sympathize with your anger over your friend, but please don't take it out on me. Like my friend said, I was just doing my job."

That was always the excuse we journalists in Fleet Street used when we were involved in some of our shameful escapades. In fact

From Tabloid To Truth

Fleet Street was dubbed "The Street of Shame." To many, we were expected to be giants with the pen. After all, weren't we following in the footsteps of William Shakespeare, H.G. Wells and Somerset Maugham? Hadn't we British, ever since Johann Gutenberg's twenty-six soldiers of lead first marched across the pages of history in the mid-fifteenth century, led the way? We "hacks" on the British tabloids, however, now appeared to the critics to have an insatiable urge to destroy all that was once great in our own country. Now it seemed we were nothing but town criers publicly proclaiming the misdeeds and misfortunes of the high, mighty, mediocre and detestable.

"But what of our misdeeds?" I had often pondered. "Who judges us?" Like one prime minister had said of the British press, "You have power without responsibility."

Another twenty minutes passed and suddenly, for some inexplicable reason, the granite-faced Scot crumbled and emotionally threw his arms around me.

"Dan, I came here tonight to kill you. Now I really like you." He fished around in his pocket and produced a ten-pound note (US$15.00) and handed it to me.

"Here, have a few drinks on me."

With that he stumbled out of the bar. I was shaking with emotion. Would he be back? Would he be waiting for me outside the pub with that knife?

"That was a close one, Dan." My friend eyed the money and said, "I think we need a drink. I think we've earned it, don't you?"

My hands were shaking helplessly as I gulped a quick drink. My friend looked at me with unusual compassion. "You've been having a rough time lately, Dan. Do you want to tell me about it?"

I did. And soon it was as if a cork had been pulled from my subconscious and it all spilled out.

"I came into Fleet Street as a Christian, thinking I could change the world," I told my colleague. "I truly believed that I could contribute something really worth while through my writing, but now I find I am getting deeper and deeper into something I can't handle."

He was aware that I was featured in the sensational Old Bailey trial of former Liberal leader John Jeremy Thorpe, who, with financier David Holmes, was accused of conspiring to kill Norman Scott. Thorpe, who pleaded not guilty to both charges, was later acquitted on all charges.

Before the trial began, a publisher had commissioned me to co-author Scott's autobiography. During the trial the judge had asked to see the contract. When he read my name on it he had uttered the immortal words, "Who and what is Dan Wooding?" The statement was faithfully reported in the national press and now my evangelical friends knew that I had agreed to work on a book with Scott. Most were horrified that I would be involved in such a project.

"Well, Dan, let me ask you, "Who and what is Dan Wooding?" That was like a knife to my heart. For I didn't know any more.

"Did you know that my life has also been threatened by another gangster and just a few weeks back? While I was out of the country, I thought an associate of this man had murdered Norma, my wife. Now, this very week, I've been told that our home phone is being tapped because of my underworld reporting. Scotland Yard wants to know what I'm talking about with these guys. Tonight, well, that was the final straw. I didn't think it would ever be like this."

My colleague looked at me as if I were just a little mad. "You still haven't got it, have you, Dan? In this game we are not paid to think."

With that he was off. I followed him out into the winter's night. As I walked out into darkened New Fetter Lane, the snow tumbled thickly out of the sky and my heart felt cold.

"God," I prayed, "If I'm not paid to think, what am I doing here? What has gone wrong with all my good intentions as a Christian? I thought, if 'all things work together for good....' I can't see any good thing coming out of my present situation."

At that moment, I didn't know what my next step should be. All I knew was that I wanted to get home to Norma and my two sons, Andrew and Peter, and enjoy being with decent people again.

I felt I needed a shower to cleanse away the filth of an evening like this.

Another problem I was dealing with was that I was harboring a whole series of grudges against people whom I believed had wronged me over the years.

One of the worst was when I was nearly sent to jail for contempt for not revealing the source of a story involving a dispute between two Christians. On another occasion, a group of Christians had threatened to sue me over something I had written in a book. My anger had begun to eat away at me like a cancer.

One night Norma talked over the situation with me. She got out her Bible and opened it at 1 Corinthians 6:1-2: "If any of you has a dispute with another, dare he take it before the ungodly for judgment instead of before the saints? ? Do you not know that the saints will judge the world? And if you are to judge the world, are you not competent to judge trivial cases?"

As we discussed the situation, I brought out my bad feelings towards an internationally known singer who had agreed to let me "ghost" his life story for a book.

"Do you remember that I gave up a considerable amount of time writing the first draft of the manuscript?" I recalled for Norma.

"Suddenly, out of the blue, came a letter from him saying he didn't want the book published after all. There was no offer of payment for my work, no real explanation. I have to admit that I've felt angry about this situation for a long time now. I've always found that the secular newspapers I've worked for pay up if they ask me to do work. Yet this man wanted me to do the book with him, then dropped it—and me."

As we spoke, I remembered telling this story to David Aikman, a Christian journalist who had worked for many years on *Time* magazine in New York. He said, "Dan, you have every right to feel hard done by. He has probably treated you very badly. But I want to point out a Scripture to you."

He pointed me Matthew 5:22-24. "Read it out loud," he suggested. "Maybe God will show you what you should do towards this man."

So I opened his Bible and began to read:

But I tell you that anyone who is angry with his brother will be subject to judgment. Again, anyone who says to his brother, 'Raca,' is answerable to the Sanhedrin. But anyone who says, 'You fool!' will be in danger of the fire of hell. "Therefore, if you are offering your gift at the altar and there remember that your brother has something against you, leave your gift there in front of the altar. First go and be reconciled to your brother; then come and offer your gift.

"You know," I said sadly to Norma, "I've never taken his advice. Maybe I should apologize to the singer for my feelings against him right now."

I quickly typed out a letter to him and sent it via his British record company.

A few days later I received a phone call from an executive of the company.

"I was in the room when he opened your letter," he told me. "He began to cry when he read what you'd written. He really appreciated you doing what you did."

The more I pondered it, the more I realized that there was a lot of poison in my system, and much of it was directed towards Christians whom I felt had wronged me.

One of those worked for Billy Graham's British office and I had given him a rough time while working on the *Sunday People*. I had even threatened to write an unflattering story about him about a petty dispute we had become embroiled in.

"Dan, the scriptural thing is to apologize to him," Norma told me. "I know it's a painful thing for you to do, but you must."

So with great trepidation I phoned him and told him how sorry I was for my attitude. I later discovered how distressed he had become over my attitude towards him.

"Thank you, brother," he told me on the phone, his voice cracking with emotion. "My big wish is that we can now become friends."

Although God was dealing with me, I was feeling more and more that my time in Fleet Street was coming to an end. I had served my apprenticeship and I felt that I should be involved in another kind of writing that was not so trivial.

I shared this one day with a close friend.

"Dan, first of all, I know from bitter experience how ruthless and cruel some Christians can be," he told me. "All those things you have shared with me I know are true, because I've experienced many of them myself. But I want to tell you something. The most important thing in the world for you at this moment is not who is right and wrong, but your personal relationship with Jesus Christ. Unless you get that right, you will always be full of bitterness and anger. God will judge those who do wrong in his own time, but he will also judge you. Are you ready for that?"

Those words were like a knife to my heart. In my confusion over the lives of those I thought I should look up to, I was forgetting my own shortcomings.

He pointed out Matthew 7:4 to me: "How can you say to your brother, 'Let me take the speck out of your eye,' when all the time there is a plank in your own eye? You hypocrite, first take the plank out of your own eye, and then you will see clearly to remove the speck from your brother's eye."

That night I got down on my knees before God and asked for forgiveness for straying so far from my original calling as a journalist. I also had to get right with Norma. I realized I had become so involved in my work and the excitement of it that I had almost completely cut her out of my life.

"Darling, it happened so easily," I said. "I got so far along the so-called success trail that I became completely selfish. I brought my work home with me. You and the boys always took second place."

She held me close and laid her hands on my head.

"Lord," she prayed, "please forgive us both for what has happened over the past few years. Help us be one again and begin to serve you as we have been called to."

Both of us were crying with happiness that we were really back with each other again.

The next day, Ray Barnett called me at the office.

"Dan, I've got another proposition for you," he said.

"Oh, yes?" I chuckled. "Last time you did that I nearly got into serious trouble in Russia. So what is it this time?"

"Oh, it's something that may cost you your life...."

When we met for lunch, he told me that he was recently in Uganda. "While I was there I discovered that Idi Amin has been conducting a real holocaust against the believers. He and his henchmen have murdered hundreds of thousands."

"I hear that much of the finance for the killing is coming from Libya and Saudi Arabia. They want Amin to set up an Islamic state and don't care to what lengths he goes to do it."

His face became serious.

"Dan, I want to ask you if you would be prepared to give up your job in Fleet Street if Idi Amin falls," he said. "Would you go to Uganda with me and get the inside story of what really happened to the church during the last few years? It could be dangerous; it will certainly mean a drop in your standard of living. But what a service you would be doing to the worldwide church of Jesus Christ. And once you've got the story, there are thousands of others around the world you could help. You could become a voice for the suffering church."

He then told me about a statement attributed to Karl Marx: "Give me twenty-six lead soldiers and I'll conquer the world."

"Dan, he meant the alphabet on a typewriter. Marx knew how powerful words can be and you can see how successful his crusade for world domination has been. Are you prepared to use your "twenty-six lead soldiers" for God?"

It was a question I had to answer soon!

20
Uganda Holocaust

It was May 1979, just weeks after Idi Amin had been routed by the Tanzanian Army and had fled to Libya to be sheltered by his friend, Muammar Khadaffy. Ray Barnett and I were heading towards Entebbe Airport to gather the story of the Uganda holocaust. We had managed to secure a book deal for the inside story of what had happened to Christians there.

"Well, Dan," said Ray, "you've gone and done it."

I smiled wryly. "Yes, I have. You know, on the last day at the paper they had a reception and all the staff sang 'All Things Bright and Beautiful' for me. I think they must have made history. I don't think a hymn has ever been sung in the *Sunday People* newsroom before."

Just then we touched down at battle-scarred Entebbe.

The passengers, mainly returning Ugandan refugees, clapped joyously as the hostess said, "Welcome home!"

In Nairobi, we approached World Vision International and they agreed to allow Ray and me to join one of their relief reconnoiters, and to travel with them in a Volkswagen Kombi that would take us on the long, hair-raising journey into the very heart of the Uganda holocaust. Joining Ray and me on that trip was Dan Brewster, an American who was relief and development associate at the World Vision office in Africa.

Now at Entebbe, we clambered down the steps of the plane to be greeted by a hot, stuffy billow of air, and I noticed a huge presence of Tanzanian troops. About three hundred yards from our plane the notorious "Whisky Run" jet stood motionless, riddled with bullets.

This Boeing 707, bearing the black, red, and yellow insignia of Uganda Airlines, used to make a weekly fourteen-hour flight to Stanstead Airport in England, where Amin's men would load it up with booze (even though they were Muslims) and other "goodies" for the killer squads. The Ugandans paid for this with cash from the sale of coffee. Often there were as much as forty tons of goods in the airplane's hold. Whisky was always a priority. It was Amin's way of buying their loyalty.

As we walked into the devastated terminal, it was amusing to see a table with a single immigration official, parked in the middle of the twisted mess. I presented my passport and before he even looked at it, he fixed me with a baleful stare and asked in an eerie, controlled voice, "Do you have any Kenyan newspapers? It gets so boring here with only two flights a day." One was from Kenya, the other Zaire.

I lamely handed him a Nairobi newspaper, so he stamped my passport. Obviously documentation didn't mean too much, as long as I had something for him to read.

When the three of us got through customs, we were met by Geoffrey Latim, a former Olympic athlete who had fled the country during Amin's reign. He was to be our guide. Latim led us to a Christian customs officer who, while being watched by a poker-faced Tanzanian soldier armed with a rifle, made a token check of our bags.

"There is no phone link with Kampala and little or no gasoline," explained Latim. "So we might be in for a long wait until a driver arrives for us. He dropped me off and said he would be back later."

Latim was right. During that time, the Christian customs official, who turned out to be from the Acholi tribe, joined us for a chat. He shared with us how God had saved his life. "I was going to be killed on April 7, 1979," he said. "But on the sixth, Entebbe was freed by the Tanzanians and my life was spared."

The man revealed that his name was on a death list found when the Tanzanians liberated the State Research Bureau headquarters at Nakasero, Kampala.

He looked sad as he told of the heartbreak of his job during Amin's rule. "I saw many people passing through customs and I knew there was no way they would reach the aircraft," he said. "They would be intercepted by the State Research men and never be heard of again. These terrible killers were all over the airport. Most of them were illiterate and had their jobs only because they were of the same tribe as Amin."

Eventually the Kombi arrived and we began the thirty-mile journey to the capital. We were stopped at several roadblocks set up by the Tanzanians, and Latim patiently explained to the positively wild-looking soldiers—most of whom were carrying a rifle in one hand, a huge looted "ghetto-blaster" playing loud, thumping disco music in the other—why we were in Uganda. Burned-out military hardware, including tanks, littered the sides of the main highway to Kampala.

Soon we were at the Namirembe Guest House, run by the Church of Uganda, but originally set up by the Church Missionary Society. It was getting dark as the van bumped its way into the grounds, which are just below the cathedral.

"You are all most welcome," said the ever-smiling manager, Naomi Gonahasa. We soon realized the incredible difficulties under which she and her staff were working. There was no running water and so it had to be brought in jerry cans from the city on the back of a bicycle, at a British pound sterling a can.

Each resident was rationed to one bottle of brownish water per day—and that was for everything. They had no gas for cooking, so it was all done on a charcoal fire. What made it even more difficult was that there were no telephones working in the entire city, so we could not alert any of Ray's contacts that we had arrived.

When we unpacked in the fading light, we heard the sounds of machine-gun fire reverberating across the city below us. Then came the sounds of heavy explosions and of screaming and wailing, which continued all through the night.

I realized that Ray had been deadly serious when he told me that this trip could cost me my life. I got down by my bed and recommitted my life to the Lord. "God," I said against a background of screaming, "I don't know what is going to happen here, but I want you to have your own way with my life, and that of Ray. We realize the dangers, but they are nothing to what our brothers and sisters here have faced over the past eight years."

As I stood up, I turned to Ray who was calmly lying on his bed, reading his Bible, and said, "A fine mess you've got me into again...."

He smiled.

"Where would you rather be—in Fleet Street, or here, serving the suffering church of Uganda?"

My look showed him that I knew I was in the center of God's will.

During our stay at the guesthouse, we became firm friends with Naomi and her husband Stephen. As we built up trust with them, they revealed their part in saving the lives of believers on the run from Amin's savage killers.

I learned from them the secret code word, which they responded to when someone came to them for sanctuary.

"This was a good hiding place from State Research people," said Stephen. "People would turn up here and as long as they knew the code word "Goodyear," we would hide them. Their food was served in their rooms. Naturally we would not let them sign the guest register in case it would be checked."

Naomi added, "We were not really frightened, because we believed that God was protecting us."

This sincere young couple, obvious targets for the State Research, were also active members of an underground church. Often believers from the Deliverance Church, one of the twenty-seven groups banned by Amin after receiving orders from Allah in dreams, would have meetings in the lounge of the guesthouse.

Next morning we had our first experience of the terrible ferocity of Amin's battle against the church during his reign of terror. We went to a church in Makerere, run by the Gospel Mission to Uganda. As we examined the bullet holes that had riddled the ceiling and the walls, I asked a member what had happened.

He told me that on April 12, 1978, Amin's wild-eyed soldiers had invaded the church and begun firing indiscriminately at the 600-strong congregation. Assistant pastor Jotham Mutebi, was on the platform and he sank to his knees in prayer.

Amid the mayhem, hundreds more quickly dropped to their knees between the pews. With upraised arms they began to praise the Lord. The sturdy red brick church was filled with a cacophony of incredible sound—a combination of prayer, praise and bullets.

Joseph Nyakairu, a member of the church orchestra, raised his trumpet to his lips and blew it as loudly as he could. The Amin soldiers thought the Christians were about to counter-attack and fled the sanctuary.

In the ensuing confusion, nearly 400 people managed to slip away from the church building. But at least 200 remained on their knees and continued to worship the Lord when the soldiers returned and continued spraying bullets everywhere. They took hold of Joseph's trumpet and threw it to the ground, spraying bullets at it. Then they "executed" the organ. The congregation knew that death could be imminent and that they were under arrest!

They were taken to the State Research Bureau headquarters at

Nakasero, and there they were mocked and told that as soon as General Mustafa Adrisi, Idi Amin's second-in-command, signed the execution order, they would all be burned alive.

The 200 sat in silent prayer and even as they prayed General Adrisi was involved in a terrible car crash in which both his legs were badly fractured. "He ended up a cripple in a wheelchair and finally Amin turned against him," said one believer.

When the signed order from Adrisi did not appear, the guards led the prisoners to the cells. They were kept behind bars for many months. Many of them were tortured, but miraculously none of them died.

As we left these incredible people, I turned to Ray and said, "I've never met believers of this caliber in my country. They certainly have much to teach us about faith and courage."

We bumped along for hours on end, having to stop regularly at roadblocks.

In Latim's hometown of Gulu, we learned the astonishing story of the burial of Archbishop Janani Luwum, who had been brutally shot in the mouth by Idi Amin himself.

Mildred Brown, an English woman who was working in the region translating the Scriptures into Acholi for the Bible Society, began to explain how Janani's body had been taken to his home village of Mucwini, near the Sudan border, for burial.

His mother, at her home, told the soldiers, "My son is a Christian. He cannot be buried here; he must be buried in the graveyard of the local church."

So the soldiers took the coffin to the picturesque tiny hilltop church for a hurried burial.

As we drank our tea, Miss Brown told us, "The soldiers had begun to dig the grave, but hadn't been able to complete the job before dark because the earth was too hard. They left the coffin in the church overnight, so they could finish the grave the next day."

Thus the hardness of the ground gave the group of believers at Mucwini the chance to gaze for the last time on their martyred archbishop. By the flickering gleam of a lamp, they saw the body of a purple-clad man. They noted there were two gun wounds, one in his neck, where the bullet had apparently gone into his mouth and out again, the other in his groin. Janani's purple robe was stained with blood, his arms were badly skinned, his rings had been stolen, and he was shoeless.

They were all gazing quietly, reverently, at the body of a martyr, a man who was killed for daring to stand up to the "black Hitler of Africa."

Even as the people gave thanks for their beloved archbishop, just one of some 500,000 victims under Amin, the government-controlled newspaper, *Voice of Uganda*, published a call for President Amin to be made emperor and then proclaimed Son of God.

Our trip into the heart of Amin's holocaust even took us into Karamoja, where naked men and boys would run across the road brandishing spears.

Famine was rife in that region. Our final memory of Karamoja was the old lady who was too weak to move, sitting silently in the village of Kotido. The woman, who appeared to be near death, squatted by her open hut to keep out of the sun's rays. She said through an interpreter that she had eaten only wild greens for two months. She displayed large folds of loose skin around her rib cage.

Famine, more than Idi Amin, had taken its toll in Karamoja.

Back in Kampala, we were able to meet up with "God's Double Agent in the President's Office." Ben Oluka, who was senior assistant secretary in the Department of Religious Affairs in Amin's office, had used his influence to save many Christian lives throughout Uganda.

But what Amin did not realize was that Ben Oluka was not only doing what be could to assist suffering believers, but was also pastoring an underground church in his home. It was a small group from the Deliverance Church, an indigenous Ugandan evangelical fellowship.

"At that time, I was working in the office that had to enforce the president's ban (against the twenty-seven Christian denominations), and secretly I was running an underground church myself," he said. "When the ban was announced, much of the church immediately went underground, and house meetings sprang up throughout the country. There is a higher power, and when government restricts freedom of worship, God's supremacy has to take over. I was personally ready for martyrdom."

And that was the feeling of millions of Ugandan believers, regardless of Amin's persecution. They were willing to die for Christ.

I returned from Uganda a different person. The courage of the Ugandan Christians will live with me forever.

"After working on a story like this, how can I ever return to Fleet Street?" I shared with Norma back home.

"You know, as I was traveling around with Ray interviewing and photographing these incredible people, I was reminded of a story I wrote all those years ago at *The Christian*."

Norma looked at me quizzically.

"Do you remember the story of Bill Howe, that spastic patient who was taught to communicate by those nurses at the hospital? They taught him to "speak" through his toe. If it hadn't been for them he would never have had a voice. I wonder if God is calling me to be a "voice" for the Christians suffering all over the world for Christ."

Norma's face creased into a huge smile. She became quiet and contemplative.

"Dan, if that is what the Lord is telling you to do, I'm thrilled. But I wonder if the excitement and lure of Fleet Street will be too much for you to resist."

21
A New Life In The New World

The imposing figure of Dr. Dale Kietzman emerged through the arrivals gate at terminal three of Heathrow Airport in London and I greeted him with a warm handshake. He had flown to the U.K. from Los Angeles to attend an Open Doors conference in Derbyshire, but was to stay with our family for a short time before I drove him there.

Dr. Kietzman had been the U.S. director of Wycliffe Bible Translators and was now working for Open Doors in the Southern California office.

I drove out of the airport in my car at breakneck speed and headed the few miles to Walton-on-Thames and noticed that Dale was holding onto his seat belt as if his life depended on it and his knuckles were white.

"Dan, could you go a little slower?" he asked.

I smiled, knowing that this man had survived all kinds of danger when he was a translator in the jungles of Peru and Brazil, but I could see that he was concerned that his life might soon end ignominiously in a tangled mess of metal on a British road.

"No problem," I smiled. "This is how we drive over here."

As the miles melted away at a more sedate pace, he asked me why we had not come over to America two years previously when invited to head up the Open Doors media department in Southern California.

"Dale, as you know, I was asked to do a couple of books for Open Doors while still living in England and I did those projects. I first went to Manila to work on *God's Smuggler to China*, with Brother David and Sarah Bruce and then *Prophets of Revolution*, a book you masterminded with Peter Gonzales. I really wanted to make the move then, but Norma and the children didn't feel a peace about it at that time."

As the blood returned to his knuckles, he said, "What about now? If I was to sponsor you, would you come now?"

"Maybe," I said, my eyes fixed on the road over Walton Bridge as I began to take the car across the majestic River Thames. "Let's see what Norma and the boys think this time."

When I asked Norma what she thought about a move, she said, "Let's pray about it," in her usual practical way. "We also need to ask the boys what they think. Only if they are in full agreement can we go!"

Norma was well aware of my desire to serve the suffering church, but this was a huge step to make. Both of our families were in the U.K. and Peter was still in school.

I had made many trips to the United States over the years and had grown to love the place, but this was different. To live in this new land was quite a step.

"Do you remember when we moved to London from Birmingham, you agreed and that worked out quite well," I told her.

"Yes, but this is thousands of miles away from home and I don't know what my mother will think," she said.

The next day, we gathered Andrew and Peter together and told them that we had been invited to move to America by Dr. Kietzman.

"We will only go if you both agree to it," said Norma.

Andrew was the first to respond. "I'm all for it," he said. "Things haven't been going to well for me here so maybe I need a fresh start." He was referring to the fact that he had been frustrated with his time at college and had felt he had somehow lost his way in life.

Peter then chimed in. "I would love to move to America," he beamed.

Before a final decision was made, I took Dale to the Swanwick Conference Centre for the conference and we spent many hours discussing the different ways we could proceed with the move across the Big Pond.

Dr. Kietzman then said, "Well, Dan, why don't you come over as soon as possible and we can make plans for the family to follow?"

I agreed and within days, I was touching down in Los Angeles and was taken to the Open Doors office in Orange, California, to meet the staff there. I immediately felt at home with the team there and then began searching for a place where we could all stay. Johnny Mitchell, one of the staff, took me house hunting and we found a duplex in Los Timbres, just up the road from the office and I signed a lease with the landlady there.

Dale then took me to meet Ernie Ching, an immigration attorney who went over with us the intricacies of immigrating to the United States. He felt it could be worked out, so I then called Norma and told her that we had a new home in our new country and I asked her to start selling everything, as we wouldn't be able to transport our furniture.

I returned to England and we had just seven weeks to clear out all of our furniture. Eventually we were left with an almost empty home and all of us slept on the floor on that final night.

We had some visitors who wanted to say goodbye to us and wish us bon voyage and they included Maurice O'Mahoney, the man I had written *King Squealer* with and Rick Wakeman.

June 28, 1982 was the day we were to fly to America and after a restless night, we gathered all of our suitcases together containing our clothes. We had arranged for many items of memorabilia to be shipped over. I gathered the family together in the living room for a time of prayer. As we stood in a circle, I prayed, "Lord, you have guided us in a miraculous way over the past few years and now we are going on another adventure for you! Please guide us in safety and prepare the way for us."

Some friends of ours then arrived to take us to Heathrow and soon we were checking in at the Pan Am desk in terminal three. I could see the faces of Andrew and Peter were flushed with excited anticipation and Norma was quietly praying. I had a few flutters of concern that maybe we were making a huge mistake, but it was too late to turn back now.

As the plane took off, I squeezed Norma's hand and said, "Maybe we will stay for a couple of years and see how it works out."

She smiled and said nothing.

After many hours of flying, we began to get close to Los Angeles and we gazed out of the window at the vast expanses of the Mojave Desert and then began to fly over the mountains that cushion the City of Angels from the desert. Then, just a few minutes later, we touched down in our new home.

After clearing immigration and customs, we all exited and were greeted by the beaming faces of Hector Tamez and his family. Hector was a Mexican Christian who had also immigrated to the

United States and was now working with Dale Kietzman in the Latin America department of Open Doors. He knew what it was like to leave his homeland and so wanted us to feel welcome.

We were in a happy daze, as we climbed into his van and were soon heading south on the 405 freeway towards Orange County. It was still light when we headed up Chapman Avenue in Orange, then turned right into Los Timbres and Hector drove into the driveway of our new home.

"Your friends at Open Doors have furnished the house for you," he said. "They have been bringing all kinds of items here for you so you will feel at home." We were near to tears as we thought of this kindness.

After dropping our suitcases in the various bedrooms, Hector said, "I want you all to join me and my family for a Mexican meal."

The next morning, as the sun rose, we went outside and were greeted by our neighbors, Dawn and Sam and Kathy and Mark. Soon other neighbors appeared, including David and Jean, who were from England.

Our first job was to find a school for Peter to attend and that was soon solved. We bought Peter a bike to ride to school. He got his first introduction to school life in America that day when a young boy shouted to him, "Your bike sucks!" as he rode onto the school grounds.

We all laughed when he recounted this over dinner.

After a few days of getting acclimatized, I went to the Open Doors office and received a warm welcome from the staff there. I was given an office and Dale and I began brainstorming on how we could bring the story of the Suffering Church to the American people.

"Maybe we could start a news service," I said one day.

"Great idea," he enthused.

So the Open Doors News Service was birthed. Dale managed to get a small budget for us to launch it, and I began to compile a media list of contacts around the world where we could send news releases.

I also began to look for radio interviews that I could do to share the vision of Open Doors. My first interview was with KYMS, a local Christian station. I spoke for an hour about our suffering brothers and sisters around the world.

Finally, the first caller was on the line. I put on my headphones and couldn't believe my ears, when a man said, "Can you tell me why the British press persecutes the Royal family?"

I realized there and then that I had a big task ahead of me in educating Americans about the persecuted church. Still, within a short time in Southern California, I felt I was home. The positive attitude of my colleagues was an encouragement for me to want to bring the message of the suffering church to American Christians.

I recalled the words of a publisher who had tried to explain why *Uganda Holocaust* had sold so few copies in the United States. "Dan," he said, "I hate to say this, but American Christians really don't care about what happened to their brothers and sisters in Uganda. They just want self-help books and need to know what is in it for them." But then another Christian told me, "If you want to reach Americans you have to use stories to illustrate your point. You won't reach Americans through their mind, but through their heart." Over the years, this has proved to be completely true. Once Americans feel an need they do want to help.

In the meantime, we knew that we needed to find Andrew a job. Dr. Ed Neteland, who had been a top man at Open Doors and had been my initial introduction to the ministry, said that he could help sell Christians books at the upcoming Full Gospel Businessman's Convention at the Anaheim Convention Center.

Andrew took the temporary position and came home each evening and regaled us with stories about "tongue-speaking men with cowboy hats and boots."

He chuckled as he said, "One of them asked me if I spoke with other tongues and then when I said I didn't, he laid hands on me and literally wrestled me to the floor in a bid to help me speak."

Each night, Andrew said he would go into the main meetings and rather than be put off by the flamboyant speakers like Oral Roberts, he actually enjoyed hearing and seeing them in action.

A few weeks after this, I was away at a Christian conference when I called home to Norma.

"Dan," she said breathlessly, "you won't believe what has just happened. Andrew told me that he wanted to accept Christ. I called Stan McCurdy [a friend that Andrew had made at the Anaheim Conference Center] and he came right over. He prayed with Andrew and he asked the Lord to forgive him of his sins and then he fell over and lay on the floor for half-an-hour and was unable to speak. He had a huge smile on his face the whole time. Then he suddenly sat up and he says he feels that he is a new person."

I could hardly contain my joy at hearing this news. Andrew had been going through a tough time in England, and now, three months after arriving in America, he had found the greatest gift anyone could have—salvation in Christ.

He was totally transformed and found a job with a local Christian organization and began to ask God what his next step should me. One day he told Norma and myself, "I believe that God wants me to join YWAM and take their DTS (Discipleship Training Course) at Holmsted Manor in England."

So, just two years after we had arrived in Southern California, we were at the airport to see him off on his long flight to the east coast and then onto London. We shed many tears as he hugged us and boarded the plane as we thought we might never see him again.

His time with YWAM was tremendous for him and he even wrote a wonderful book about his experiences called, *I Wonder if Chocolate Kills Brain Cells*. It was to be the first of seven books that he has written. After his YWAM experience, he attended Capernwray Hall, a Christian college in the Lake District of England.

In the meantime, Peter was growing up fast and was becoming a handful as he threw himself into the California lifestyle of drinking and partying. But soon, we also saw a great blessing in his life. At 15, he was just beginning his spiritual journey.

Norma and I had been attending Calvary Chapel of Costa Mesa, pastored by Chuck Smith, a unique church that had grown out of sixties and seventies hippie movement. Each Saturday night, they would hold a Christian rock concert and then have a speaker to share the Gospel.

Peter agreed to join me for these concerts and each time he came he was more open to finding out more. Then, the morning of the day we were going to see the Joe English Band (English had played with Paul McCartney's Wings), I had a strong impression that Peter was going to become a Christian that night.

After enjoying the music, he sat intently as the preacher told how it was possible for individuals to receive Christ into their life. He then asked everyone to bow their heads and close their eyes, and invited those who wanted to make that commitment to raise their hand. When I opened my eyes, I asked Peter if he'd done it, and he said "yes." We couldn't help but both sit there beaming at each other.

He was then asked to come to the church altar with scores of others. I jumped out of my seat and stood by him, my arms around his shoulder and I felt a tear slip down my cheek as he prayed the sinner's prayer.

Unfortunately, for the next five years, Peter was torn between church-life and the California partying lifestyle. It all came to a head when the police caught him for underage drinking and he had to go to court. Fortunately, this was a wake-up call for him, and just weeks later during a Bible study at Calvary Chapel, Peter got down on his knees and made a recommitment to Christ, and never looked back after that night.

So, six year after we arrived in the United States, Peter also joined YWAM and took the same DTS course at Holmsted Manor as his brother. He then traveled the world sharing Christ with people of many nations.

Still, there was the problem of helping to make the American Church aware of the Suffering Church, so I continued to write for the news service and also appear on various radio and TV shows. But somehow there was a barrier that I couldn't penetrate.

One day, I was speaking with the leader of the National Religious Broadcaster's Convention about my concerns about the circus that much of American Christianity seemed to be.

"I look around this convention and all I see is broadcasters with huge egos who don't seem to care about what is happening to our brothers and sisters around the world," I told him. "It's like a three-ring circus."

He smiled and said, "Dan, you are not going to change it, so why not use it. You can make a difference by just going on the media shows and talking about the Persecuted Church. American Christians are not callous, but they don't really know what is happening. Just tell them the truth and they will respond."

His advice was just what I needed to hear. But would I be able to do it?

22
Blurred Images And Lebanon

I squinted my eyes to look at Norma, but all I could see were blurred images of her pretty face. "Are you all right?" she asked anxiously.

I paused for a moment then let it all pour out. "Well, love, I didn't want to worry you but I haven't been able to see properly—and it's getting worse by the hour."

Before she could respond, I continued my tale of woe, "Also I keep drinking gallons of coke and then dashing to the bathroom. On top of that I've got a rash that just won't clear up."

Without a moment's hesitation, she said, "I think you should see the doctor, Dan. Something's radically wrong."

I suppose I had hoped these problems would clear up, but now I was faced with what seemed like a hopeless situation. If I allowed this to continue it could only get worse, yet if I went to the doctor, he might tell me that I had an incurable disease—a "verdict" I did not want to hear.

I finally visited my doctor and, as I described my disturbing symptoms, he decided to take a blood test.

"You have all the classic symptoms of diabetes," he said. "The test will tell us if you do have it."

"If I do, does that mean I will have to inject myself with insulin?" I asked, shivering at the thought of sticking a needle into my arm several times a day.

"No, Dan," he said gently. "I would guess that you have what is called non-insulin-dependent or adult-onset diabetes. You won't be alone. Many millions of people suffer from this."

But then he went on to say, "Complications such as gangrene, kidney disease, blindness, heart attack and strokes are associated with diabetes. It is also the most likely cause of new cases of blindness.

"However, Dan, if we catch it in time, as in your case, the chances of developing these complications are greatly reduced."

He looked at me and said that this kind of diabetes strikes

mainly people over forty, especially the overweight. I was forty-two and certainly carrying more than my fair share of flab.

"You're going to have to lose quite a few pounds, and also I'll give you some medicine, that is if the blood test proves positive."

It did! The laboratory discovered that I had more than three times the blood-sugar level than is normal. At first I began to be angry with God. Why should I get such an illness when I was finally in his full-time service? What possible good could come out of this?

Also, having a hearty appetite, I wasn't sure how I was going to cope with a food intake which would be one-third of what I was used to.

"Just think," said Norma, as I half-heartedly picked at the bowl of Grape Nuts and milk set before me at breakfast, "The Bible teaches us that our body is the temple of the Holy Spirit and once you have lost all that weight, you will have a much better temple for the Lord to dwell in."

At first I felt an almost constant hunger, and I found my nerves often stretched to their limit. But there were compensations. My eyesight was getting better, my thirst was more normal, the skin problem was clearing up. I began to feel that I might enjoy being skinny again—something I hadn't been for twenty years.

Then, just one week after I had been diagnosed as diabetic, I felt a frightening stabbing pain in my chest. Norma noticed my deathly white appearance as I walked through the door.

"I think I'm having a heart attack," I winced as the pain carved up my chest.

Within thirty minutes I was in the Intensive Care unit of a local hospital, totally immobilized and attached to several machines. Heart specialists frantically checked the instruments as I was put onto an I.V. drip.

However, strangely enough, I felt a real peace. "Lord," I whispered to the accompaniment of the electronic bleeps of the cardiac monitor recording my heartbeat. "I might be joining you very soon and I'm ready! Whatever you have in mind for me, I'll accept it."

As I lay there, I let my mind drift back to eighteen months previously when we had packed up our lives into six suitcases and headed for Southern California, full of hope and excitement.

It was quite an experience getting acclimatized to life in the United States and launching the Open Doors News Service, which began with a mailing list of about 100 and was soon being sent each month to 1,000 newspapers and media outlets around the world.

I enjoyed the challenge of sharing the vital message of the suffering church through the American mass media, including the 700 Club, the Trinity Broadcasting Network, the Moody Radio Network and eventually, being appointed as a stringer for the UPI Radio Network which is based in Washington, D.C.

But now, here I was, in the American hospital with, it seemed, my career about to come to an abrupt and tragic end. With diabetes and now heart trouble, there was no way I could continue to report from the hot spots of this world. My next assignment, to the most dangerous country on earth, Lebanon, was definitely off. I had agreed to go there with a team of doctors and paramedics organized by the Carlsbad-based group, Christian Emergency Relief Teams (CERT).

After twenty-four hours my condition stabilized and, much to my relief, I was told that I had not had a heart attack. The illness wase linked to the massive change my body was now undergoing through diet and medication.

"I was supposed to go to Lebanon at the end of the week," I told the doctor who had diagnosed my diabetes. "But I've told my wife to cancel the trip."

I nearly did have a heart attack when he told me that I was wrong in doing that.

"Dan, you should go! You will be with expert medical people while you're there. The worse thing you can do is to consider yourself an invalid." He exuded that traditional paternal air that you associate with a doctor.

"It's as if you've fallen off a horse. You need to get straight back on and start again."

I didn't like to tell him that it wasn't just the diabetes that concerned me, but the mindless killing that was going on in that war-torn land. Maybe I would survive this situation, only to be cut down by a bullet or a bomb in violence-crazy Lebanon.

But I had also to consider that God had spared me from death in a bombing in El Salvador, freed me from prison in Nigeria and protected me during my time in Uganda.

So, with great trepidation, I decided I would go to Lebanon, whatever the consequences.

From Tabloid To Truth

The fourteen-year-old crippled Lebanese boy maneuvered himself on his crutches towards me, then stopped in his tracks and held out his hand.

"Welcome," he said in faltering English, adding with a faint smile, "You like my gun?" With that he gestured towards the pistol secured in a holster at his side.

I smiled weakly, not quite knowing how to respond. I really shouldn't have been surprised. This was southern Lebanon in the summer of 1983, where almost everyone owned at least one firearm and twenty private armies operated apparently at will.

To one of the team, Dr Tom Suard, Lebanon was all quite a shock, despite the fact that he regularly treated knife and gunshot wounds resulting from gang warfare in L.A. ghettos. "Working in the hospital in Los Angeles, we are rather detached," said the doctor who was just starting his medical career. "They bring the injured in and we take care of them. We're not out in the field. We don't have the bombs bursting. We're not on the cutting edge. We're well protected. Lebanon is like being on the frontline."

Tom was one of a unique team of twenty doctors, paramedics, and pastors whom I had joined in this "invasion" of southern Lebanon as part of a love-strike to a country that has seen little but hate over the previous few years. Each individual had raised a fairly large sum money to cover the cost of the trip. It was organized in conjunction with Lebanon Aid, an organization started shortly after the Israelis invaded Lebanon in June 1982.

The group split up into four teams of medics and pastors, and each was to work in villages and cities treating the sick and also presenting the gospel to all who would listen. Some worked with Lebanon Aid medical vans, others in more permanent clinics.

The medics diagnosed what was wrong, administered what treatment they could, and then prayed with each patient. At the same time they kept an eye on my condition, but, fortunately, my health held out.

The most experienced doctor in the party, John Merriman, said, "The Lebanese we saw didn't have any war-related injuries except stress."

The widespread stress was not really surprising, as it was estimated that at that time the civil war between Lebanese Christians and Muslims had claimed more than 30,000 lives. That was on top of the 19,000 killed in the fighting in the previous twelve months between Israel and the Palestine Liberation Organization.

Dr. Merriman and Dr. Suard presented two extremes of background and experience on this Lebanon mission. Dr. Merriman was widely traveled. He had been on short-term medical missions to Central America, including Guatemala, while Tom Suard, on the other hand, had never been overseas before.

Both, however, had the same aim: to bring some of Christ's love to this ravaged land. And to all participants, Lebanon was a land of surprises. In some ways it was like the Wild West except, tragically, much of the killing was taking place in the name of God. It's a country where the different brands of Christianity and Islam, led by their armed feudal chieftains, try to outdo each other with their vile atrocities.

One CERT team member was kidnapped, taken to a Christian Falangist meeting, and then subjected to propaganda. "It was something out of a James Bond film," one paramedic told me. "We were all put in a vehicle and driven there at speeds of up to 70 miles per hour.

"When we got to the meeting we found the area heavily guarded. They made sure that nobody was following us, and then we went into the meeting. There were guns lying around everywhere, while others had them hidden in their clothing."

Several of us, on one occasion, got another insight into the situation. A Lebanese doctor took us into the dangerous Shouf Mountains. The doctor administered his medicine in villages controlled by the mystical Druze sect (a group derived from Islam but differing strongly from it). We were the first westerners to enter the area in ten years. "I'm probably the only Christian who could come out of this area alive," the doctor told us as an armed Druze militiaman checked us out as we sat in our vehicles high in the mountains.

The doctor later told me, "I know there is so much hatred in my country, but I can only follow the example of Jesus who showed love and reconciliation to all. Love is the only answer to the problems here."

The CERT team soon realized that the real long-term answer to Lebanon's problems is a spiritual one. So in both small and larger ways the team members tried to share the gospel with all with whom they came in contact.

Mike Landrum, a medical student, kept it simple. He had a Gideon Bible with him in which John 3:16 was printed in Arabic. "We were in a predominately Muslim village," he told me. "I took out that little Bible and showed the verse to some men waiting to be seen by the doctor. They read it out loud. It was a tremendously rewarding thing for me to just stand and watch them read that verse of Scripture. It was the best I could do."

Jon Courson, a pastor of Jacksonville Calvary Chapel in Oregon (now at Calvary Chapel Costa Mesa), was able to reach out to a wider audience through an interpreter. He addressed several home meetings and one day spoke near a medical van to a large crowd of villagers. Many accepted Christ during his meetings.

Lebanon Aid had been taking in more teams of pastors from Great Britain and the United States. They were encouraged to stay for a few weeks and live in Lebanese homes.

"Southern Lebanon is wide open for the gospel at this time," said Bible teacher Mac Kingsbury from England. We met him as he was going house-to-house in both Christian and Muslim villages. "There is a great hunger here and people respond readily to love. They have been so starved of it over the past few years. I would definitely encourage others to come here, not so much to do Bible teaching, but evangelism."

Nasr Audi, former Chief Deputy to the speaker of the Lebanese Parliament and then President of Lebanon Aid, said that there had never been a better time for Christians to take Arabic Bibles into southern Lebanon.

Nasr told me that he had committed his life to Jesus Christ as the war between Israel and the PLO raged in his country. Ray Barnett, who had just started Lebanon Aid in the country, led him to Christ.

"Many people here were like me. They believed they were Christian because they belonged to what is called a Christian family," said Nasr. "But they have to realize, like I did, that what is needed is a personal relationship with Jesus Christ. And the best way they can get to know him is through the Bible."

Nasr said that most "Christian" Lebanese do not own a Bible. "They leave it to the local priest to interpret the Scriptures for them. We have already been able to place 2,500 Bibles, but that is hardly scratching the surface," he continued. "There are some

580,000 people in southern Lebanon, and I would like to see each one of them own a Bible."

The director of CERT, David Courson, said that this trip showed something very important to the people of Lebanon. "Jesus instructed us to come and heal in his name. This is what I believe we have been able to do in a small way," he declared. "There is a saying we have in CERT: "People don't care how much you know until they see how much you care."

The whole experience of Lebanon was faith building for me, because I realized that my predicament was relatively minor compared with the Lebanese.

I also began to realize that we are called to be servants—whatever the cost may be to us. We are not called to be whining complainers, something I had become for a short time. Our example was Jesus himself.

Since first discovering that blurred vision is not always bad, I have learned to be more dependent on Jesus and, much to Norma's delight, and I've lost quite a portion of the old Dan Wooding. In fact, I'm over 48 pounds lighter.

"I guess that day my vision went fuzzy really did help me to get my faith more directly in focus," I shared with Norma recently.

She smiled quietly to herself, opened her Bible and read to me a verse that the Lord had given her from Jeremiah 18:6: "Behold like the clay in the potter's hand, so are you in my hand."

She turned her watery eyes on mine and said, "When I first read this you were still in the hospital. It's as if the Lord was saying, "Don't worry, everything is going to be fine. I'm just doing some remodeling in Dan's life."

Then looking at me, she grinned, "So far I think he's done a very good job... I think you must be the first person to immigrate to America and lose weight!"

As an added confirmation from the Lord that I should continue with my writing, despite my illness, I heard the following year that the article I wrote for the California magazine *Contemporary Christian* on the Lebanon trip—"Bibles & Bandages"—won first prize in the reporting section of the Evangelical Press Association (of the USA) in its "Higher Goals" contest.

It began to seem to me as if the needs of our Christian brethren were never-ending and my work with the Open Doors News Service meant my bags were always packed, ready for the next assignment.

23
The Greater The Sorrow, The Closer To God

Military music blared loudly from the radio in our compartment of the Trans-Siberian Express. We were leaving Moscow's Yaroslavi Station to begin the world's longest railway journey: to and then across Siberia.

It was February 1985, and I was there to research an article for the Open Doors News Service. I would be traveling 3,200 miles in freezing winter conditions—and that was only half way across the enormous expanses of Siberia, a wasteland where up to two million Soviets had been sent to labor camps for a variety of reasons ranging from crime and political intrigue to religious persecution. Siberia is an area that is larger in size than either China or the United States.

Down the length of this snake-like electric train, Russians, Georgians, Siberians, Americans and British started unpacking their belongings from battered suitcases and began to turn their two, four and six-bed compartments into temporary homes. Yuri, an over-sized friendly bear of a man, just a few compartments back, started to peel off his heavy clothes and put on the blue pajama jacket he would wear for the rest of the trip. Others, in different compartments, began unraveling packages containing loaves of bread, hunks of cheese and generous supplies of vodka.

"I think I'm going to enjoy this after all," commented one of the members of our group, which consisted of ten Americans and one British exile. I had joined them for this two-week visit to the Soviet Union, actually surprised I had been granted a visa after the "Road Block to Moscow" incident back in 1972.

The journey had got off to an unusual start. As we stood at the wind-blown Moscow station waiting for our luggage to be loaded on board, fists had flown furiously just a few yards away as two porters, dressed like grizzly bears, exchanged blows for the privilege of loading the baggage.

With hostilities finally ending—not without bloodshed—their

colleagues separated the warring porters, and we were finally allowed to board the Rossiya (Russia) Express. We settled into our two-berth, first-class compartments (yes, there is a class system even in the supposedly classless society of the Soviet Union), and although not large, they were actually quite comfortable. Each had upholstered berths, a table, mirror, radio, heating (or air conditioning in the summer), and an attendant-call button.

As we plunged deeper and deeper into the frozen wastes of Siberia, I stood in the corridor, staring out of the window, watching the full moon, and reflecting on the case of the Vashchenko and Chymakalov families. They had made the reverse journey in June 1978 from their home in the coal-mining town of Chernogorsk, 2,000 miles east of Moscow. This group of Siberian Pentecostalists, who were to play a great role in my own life, wanted to emigrate from the Soviet Union so they could practice their faith free from the persecution of communist authorities.

Their date with fate was June 27, 1978. In the party wanting freedom was Peter Vashchenko, a man of medium height in his mid-fifties, with dark hair and moustache, and wearing a neat dark suit. Among the 150,000 Pentecostals living in the Soviet Union, Peter had been a leading advocate of religious freedom since 1960. At his side were his wife, fair-haired Augustina, and four of their children, Lida, Lyuba, Lilia and John. Another boy, Timothy, came with his mother, Maria Chymakalov.

The costs of being Christians in Siberia were high for the Vashchenkos. Lida, especially, suffered terribly. Her family insisted on bringing her up as a Christian and did not want to send her to the local school where atheism was taught. So her father made a secret place for the children to hide. "Sometimes the police would make lightning searches," she recalled. "When they came at night our hearts were beating so loudly that it seemed they would hear us upstairs. If they came at daytime, we would hide there frozen with terror. The memory of it makes me shiver all over."

For five long months, despite constant searches by the police, Peter was able to keep the secret. Then one day a police car came by and the officers caught the children playing in front of the house. Someone had forgotten to keep lookout. Lida ran into the barn and scrambled away under a large wooden box, but was discovered. "A policeman jumped on my leg and finally grabbed me. I screamed and then the rest came and took me."

Lida, then eleven, was placed for a while in the Abakan State Orphanage—the home of runaways, orphans and outlaws. "It was a very difficult period of my life. I did not try to find friends, because I spent my days in secret loneliness and in tears. For me it was if I had been buried alive."

Then again, when she was seventeen, Lida was taken from her parents, along with her three younger sisters, Lyuba, Nadaya and Vera, and placed in another children's home. Her parents were imprisoned in Moscow because they had tried again to talk to the Americans about their planned emigration to the U.S. Peter was, imprisoned for one year and underwent investigations in a psychiatric hospital. Augustina was imprisoned for more than two years.

"After a brief stay in the state-run children's home in Krasnoyarsk," said Lida, "we were sent to Kansk. We were taken to the plane in a special vehicle escorted by police. When the plane arrived at Kansk airport, a security truck was waiting near the exit. There were comments from astonished people such as, "What kind of children can they be, to be in the hands of the police?"

"But how could they know who we really were? What criminal needs six to eight policemen to keep him at bay? Many times during my twenty-seven years under Soviet control I have had a police escort, but I still can't get used to it. Every time I am surrounded by police, I feel ashamed and want to cry, 'Listen, all of you! Don't look at me like that! I'm not a criminal. I haven't earned your reproachful glances and degrading comments.'"

"But then," said Lida, "I think of Jesus Christ, and I am reminded that he didn't want to answer, not that he had no answer. He knew that his questioners were interested neither in the questions nor in the answers. They wanted to sentence him, not only by their questions, but also by distorting his answers."

Employment for Lida was always a problem. As a Christian, she was a marked person for the authorities. For instance, when she was just twenty-four years old, she refused a position as a store superintendent, because it involved giving lectures on atheism to the staff. Instead, she went to work as an orderly in a maternity hospital in Chernogorsk.

Across the street was a women's aid service and a place where abortions were carried out daily by the state. Sometimes babies that had been aborted late and had survived would be carried across to the hospital. Although they were fed, they were not placed in the intensive care unit. Naturally it was heartbreaking for Lida to care for such "tortured babies."

One day in 1975, Lida asked if she could look after one of the aborted babies who had survived. She took the baby that she named Aaron home and cared for him and eventually legally adopted him. When Aaron was just five months old, the authorities took the baby back for medical experiments.

"They got the mother to agree to experimental surgery on his brain and also to test new drugs," said Lida. "Normally, they would do this type of experimenting on animals, but they chose to do it on Aaron instead."

"When he died, they buried him in a local cemetery and I went there to dig him up to get the evidence about the way he was killed."

This was just another example of the intentional cruelty the authorities leveled at Christians in the Soviet Union.

So it was not surprising that the single-minded Vashchenkos had been trying to emigrate since 1962. An attempt to discuss their emigration with U.S. officials in 1978 was to be frustrated. Despite the fact that Peter was clutching a letter from the embassy inviting him to come and discuss his family emigration, the Russian guards would not let them through. As a heated discussion ensued, the guards began to beat sixteen-year-old John with their clubs.

While this was happening the rest of the family ran past the surprised guards and took refuge in the lobby of the embassy.

"We ran like we were escaping from a wild beast," Lida told me. "For we knew that if we were caught it would be prison and maybe even death. As we ran we kept shouting at the top of our voices, 'Help! Help!'"

"When we first arrived, they tried different ways to persuade us to leave the embassy, but we knew that leaving would be death for us.

"Then, an official at the embassy made a list and hung it on the wall saying that if volunteers would like to feed us, would they please sign up. So each day these kind people would bring us food. It was a different family each day."

Eventually, the embassy cooperated with them and gave them a basement room to live in. They all lived in a cramped twelve by twenty feet room behind the embassy barbershop. They could look out through the iron grill at the booted feet of the Soviet guards and beyond to the grinding traffic of Moscow's Tchaikovsky Street.

So began what was to be one of the longest "sit-ins" in history. It was a gesture that was to strike at the very heart of the Kremlin. The "Seven" became something of a worldwide cause célèbre, with marches and vigils taking place around the world for them.

I was told of their case during a visit to Seattle when I met with Dr. Kent Hill, a history professor at Seattle Pacific University, in the spring of 1981. "Dan, I was in Moscow at the time they rushed into the American Embassy and they became my close friends," Hill told me at his home. "They are wonderful people whom I spent many hours with. I speak Russian and we would have Bible studies together."

Hill asked me, "Could you launch a campaign on their behalf in England? There is a stalemate. It seems the U.S. and Russians are just not talking to each other on this case. Maybe if a third country got involved, that could break the stalemate."

Those few words were the challenge that launched the "Campaign to Free the Siberian Seven," which mobilized thousands of British Christians to action on behalf of these seven courageous Christians.

When I returned to England, I shared Hill's challenge with Peter Meadows, Publishing Director of *Buzz* magazine, Tony Collins, then editor at Hodder & Stoughton, and Danny Smith, a journalist friend, who was to spearhead the campaign in Britain.

Within weeks, the campaign had been launched, thousands had signed a petition on their behalf at Spring Harvest, a Christian convention, and more than 100 Members of Parliament and the House of Lords had pledged their support to the cause. Trafalgar Square was packed with demonstrators on behalf of the Siberians.

I joined American and British Christians in leading a long march of 3,000 people through London to the Soviet Embassy in Kensington Palace Gardens, London, where an all-night vigil took place.

There were press conferences, badges, petitions, rallies, but most of all, there was prayer. The campaign spread around the world from Britain and even returned to the United States where thousands of American Christians showed their solidarity with the "Siberian Seven."

But still the Kremlin showed no compassion until Augustina

began a hunger strike on Christmas Day, 1981, and Lida began her twenty-eight day fast shortly afterwards. Their actions finally captured world headlines and began the incredible turn-around in the Kremlin's thinking towards these seven Christians. The Soviets began to worry about the bad publicity a death in the embassy would cause. Especially harmful to them was an article, which appeared in Time magazine that was, headlined "Deadly Game in a U.S. Embassy, Soviet Pentecostalists try to win freedom with a hunger strike."

Lida was desperately ill when she was finally taken from the embassy in the glare of the world's press to Moscow's Botkin Hospital. After her life was saved by Soviet doctors during fourteen days in hospital, she was sent back to her home in Chernogorsk, to be, once again, reunited with her other eleven brothers and sisters.

Lida made it clear that she did not desire to risk her life. "It was a fast to ask the Lord to intercede on our behalf," she said.

Lida felt this "two-pronged" strategy really paid off. "I knew that many non-Christians would not understand the fast 'to the Lord' but would understand the hunger-strike aspect. And they did! Many politicians understood the word "hunger-strike" and paid attention to what was happening."

Lida described the pathos in the embassy before she was carried out. "I got on my knees and began praying. Those around me began to feel this might be the last time they would see me. So they began to ask for forgiveness for anything they may have done against me."

She said, "I looked up at them and smiled weakly. They all seemed to be towering above me. I just wanted to pray, but they all wanted my forgiveness. I was kneeling on the floor and they just kept asking for forgiveness!"

When Lida was transported home to Chernogorsk in February 1982, it was ironically a KGB officer who helped her.

"As I walked from the plane down the stairway, I was still very light-headed and my head started spinning and I almost fainted," she recalled.

"It was a KGB man who held me up. I think he was afraid that I would fall over and then the world would say that they had injured me."

When she got to her home, it was a difficult time at first for her.

"The little children didn't recognize me because I looked so different," recalled Lida. "I think they were a little scared of how I looked. But next day they got braver and began asking among themselves who I was. Soon they began following me everywhere, even to the bathroom! They'd stand at the door and wait until I came out.

"If I went to lie down on the bed, they would sit down on my bed and just look at me. Often I would lie there so weak and fall asleep and they would throw their arms and legs about me and go to sleep too."

One extraordinary fact that Lida revealed was that when she returned to Chernogorsk, she made an American flag with thirteen stars (that's all the material she could get hold of), and put it on the roof of their home.

"Whenever the KGB came to try and pull it down, our Alsatian dog would go for them," she smiled. "We wanted to show them that we still wanted to emigrate and that we believed that America was the home of the free."

Eventually, the prayers and campaigning paid off, and Lida was freed in April 1983. On June 27th, fifteen members of the Vashchenko family were allowed to leave for the West, followed shortly afterwards by fifteen members of the Chymakalov family, including Maria and Timothy. They clutched Russian Bibles given out by their American supporters and one of them wore a T-shirt with the Bible verse inscribed on it, "If God is for us, who can be against us?"

Martyn Halsall of the London *Guardian*, said, "When I saw Peter Vashchenko coming down the steps of the plane in Vienna, I was surprised to see how small he was. A small man in a crumpled brown suit, smiling, because he had taken on the Soviet government and won."

All have settled in the United States, though Peter has since died from cancer.

After Lida arrived in the West, she first of all headed for Israel. It was there that I first met her. We stood together as she gazed wistfully onto the pond-like surface of the Sea of Galilee. Suddenly her taut face creased into a broad smile.

Then I asked her if over the past five years her personal relationship with God had deepened. She answered, "We have a hymn in Russia which says, 'The greater the sorrow, the closer is God.'"

From Tabloid To Truth

I again gazed out of the window, at the frozen expanses reflected in the moonlight and felt closer to the Christians of Siberia—and closer to God!

Great happiness came to Lida on August 2, 1986, when she married Egyptian Christian George Gergis whom she met at an English class in California, where she now lives. I attended her wedding and for a time we lived just around the corner from her new home in Garden Grove, California.

24
Saved From
"A Highway To Hell"

Barry Taylor looked like a rock star with long hair and earrings, but in fact he was the senior pastor of a church in Lake Arrowhead, located in the beautiful mountains of the San Bernardino Mountains, southern California.

When we first met at his church where I was taping a TV program, little did I realize the impact Barry would have on my life and ministry. He told me that he was from Huntington in England, and had been a roadie with Black Sabbath, Ozzy Osbourne's infamous rock band and then had joined AC/DC as their roadie/drum engineer for their "Highway to Hell" tour of the United States.

I began to unravel his extraordinary story when we began working on his life story for a book called "Singing in the Dark," which was later published in the U.K. by Kingsway and in the US by Dove Publishing.

Here are a few excerpts that will introduce you to Barry, then nicked named "The Skull" for his looks and dress, and his story—in his own words:

I was dressed in my usual attire—a black motorcycle jacket, black T-shirt and jeans, and three dangling earrings, not black, but silver, attached to two rather pink ears.

While the AC/DC lighting and sound equipment was being unloaded in Phoenix, Arizona, from our trucks by the union crew, I decided to use the spare time to go on a mission; to locate a bookstore where I could buy a Bible. This was definitely not an everyday occurrence for me, but something I felt I had to do for the sake of Derek, my poor deluded friend.

I found a Christian bookstore close by and, for some reason as I walked through the door, I felt scared. However, I was sure that I was not as apprehensive as the lady behind the counter. I'm sure she had not had too many "screaming skulls" walking into the shop before.

From Tabloid To Truth

"Do you have a Bible I could buy, Luv?" I asked her as she cowered behind the counter.

There was a long pause as she gazed, her mouth agape, at me. Perhaps she thought that I was casing the joint to rob it. Little did she know that underneath this dark exterior was a wimpy Englishman.

She eventually overcame her fear and brought out a selection of Bibles for me to choose from. I left the shop carrying a large Open Study Bible under my arm. I then stopped at a nearby liquor store and bought a copy of Rolling Stone magazine.

The large guy behind the counter there looked strangely at me as he spotted my leather-bound Bible.

Excuse me, sir," I asked hesitantly, "do you have a big bag to put these items in."

He looked at me as if I should be locked up, but handed over a large brown bag into which I put the Bible and magazine. When I climbed on board the tour bus, I put my Bible in a safe place by my bunk and resumed my career with the band. I reassured myself that the Bible wasn't for me, but to help my friend Derek. He was definitely in serious trouble having become what is commonly known as a "religious nut."

We had come to Arizona by way of Los Angeles and, for the first time in a couple of years, I had the opportunity, or maybe misfortune, of spending time with Derek [a former roadie with AC/DC who had been converted to Christ] there.

I knew I would have some time off in Los Angeles and before arriving there I had called Derek from Chicago to tell him of my imminent arrival. I knew he was a new Christian but I figured he was still Derek, and so he surely must have had Los Angeles pretty well mapped out and knew were all the good times could be had.

I arranged to stay with him rather than with the band at a hotel. It was a big mistake. I knew something was wrong as soon as he picked me up. We were waiting for the garage attendant to bring up his car from the underground parking structure when, after our hello's, he said, "Barry, there's something I've got to tell you."

I mentally ducked, guessing he was going to lay it on me.

"I don't know if you know it or not, but the world we live in is in a big mess and it's not going to' last forever." His usually good-humored face was still and serious and composed.

Momentarily nonplussed, I passed on replying, but thought to myself,

"Big deal. Just so long as it lasts as long as I'm on it."

Derek seemed impervious as to my reaction to his preaching and ploughed on with his diatribe:

"And whether you believe it or not Barry, one day Jesus Christ is going to return for His Church." He was now launched into his own monologue. "And if you're not in His Church, you're going to be in big trouble."

I realized I was already in "big trouble." I'd committed myself to spend a few days with a man who was obviously in need of some serious psychiatric help. If I'd have had more backbone, I would have said good-bye forever right there and then and happily never conversed with my friend again. But I had a flaw in my character of never wanting to upset anybody, so I figured I would just have to ride this one out.

Barney's Beanery in Hollywood was a trendy hang out for rock and rollers as well as "wanna-be's" and this was where Derek took me one day. As I sunk my teeth into one of their famous burgers, I tried to keep the conversation off the subject of Jesus Christ and magnanimously plied Derek with many questions about life in LA Derek turned each answer around to having some reference to the Bible.

After an excruciatingly embarrassing journey, we arrived at his home in the Hollywood Hills. He lived with a small group of other people. Surely, I hoped, were not religious nuts as well.

After a few moments of introduction, I realized from all the "hallelujah's" and "praise God, Brother, we're glad you're here," that Derek was not the only one in need of help. My mood had abruptly switched to tired irritation. They were all so happy and their joy made me somehow aware of my own distinct lack of it.

Those couple of days were worse than any chemistry class I had attended back in school in Huntingdon. In fact, they were worse than anything I'd ever endured anywhere. The people weren't pushy in trying to ram their beliefs down my throat, it was just that they did believe and that affected the whole way that they lived. Their relationship with Jesus Christ was as real and valid as any of their other relationships and obviously, to me, it had provided them with a joy and a zest for life that made me angry.

I was even dragged along to a Bible study in a house somewhere in Los Angeles. It was incredibly boring. The place was jam-packed with smiling Californians clutching Bibles, closing their eyes and lifting their hands and singing choruses. The house was so full that I spent the evening trying to peer through a crack in the kitchen door to catch a glimpse of the guy who was teaching from the Bible. Even I had to admit that his message was a lot more relevant and real than anything else I'd ever heard during my brief stint at church in England.

That short entanglement with Christianity had come about when I had joined the Boy's Brigade. My motive was that I wanted to learn to play the drums, but I soon grew tired of the whole thing when I discovered that there was a pathway that had to be traveled in order to get your hands on the drumsticks. And that involved learning first to play the bugle, not exactly a rock and roll instrument.

Fortunately, my three-day Los Angeles nightmare ended and Arizona beckoned. In my heart, I knew that this was the last time I would ever see Derek again. I was prepared to bear the bad tidings of his total insanity to all my friends in England.

As Derek dropped me off at the hotel before we left, he handed me a couple of books and said, "I want you to take these and give them a read. They really meant a lot to me and opened up my eyes."

I took them and glanced down at their titles. They were, *Mere Christianity* by C.S. Lewis and *The Late Great Planet Earth* by Hal Lindsey.

"Thanks Derek," I muttered, trying to be as nice as possible but, thinking all the time, if I took them he'd shut up and not embarrass me any more.

With a deep sense of relief, I boarded the tour bus and left for the sanctuary of life on the road. As we drove through the desert to Arizona, I thumbed through the books, more out of boredom than anything else. They weren't actually as tiresome as I thought they would be. In fact, they expressed some realities that I had never considered before. They seemed to be talking about a God who was at work in the earth, who was intimately involved with the humans on it and, from their perspective, he had a plan. I stuffed them at the bottom of my bag and resumed my life with the band.

However hard I tried, I just couldn't leave them alone. I told myself it was because I was concerned about Derek's mental health, feeling that "normal" people did not have to get so worked up about God and all that religious 'stuff. I resolved that I would make it a personal mission to disprove from the Bible what these men were saying and then prove to Derek that this Christianity business wasn't really necessary.

My assignment became all consuming. I spent every spare moment taking these books and their references to the Bible and attempting to show the futility of their thesis. The one thing I had remembered from my English class at school was that it's very easy to take things out of context and make things say what you want, so I figured I'd put their quotes back in context and get the real picture.

Strangely enough, the more I tried to disprove one of these writers, the more I found myself agreeing with him. After a while I decided that maybe I should just forget the books and study the Bible for myself so that I could, at least, let Derek know that I'd done a good job of trying to accept what he showed.

As the AC/DC bus traversed the nation and everybody else continued with their usual an-tics from consuming drugs to watching porno films, I ploughed through the Old Testament.

I wasn't too impressed.

This God seemed to wreak an awful lot of destruction, wiping out nations, killing people, and I, of course, had my standard arguments, such as, "If God is God and He is a God of love," which Derek was continually telling me, then how come there is injustice and people starving?"

Another was, "How is that evil men are triumphing over good?" and "How come there is so much suffering in the world?"

None of my Bible reading seemed to be providing any answers.

I read one day of a French philosopher, Emile Caillet, who, while sitting in the trenches during World War I, reflected on the misery, despair and emptiness of his life and longed to find a book that, in his words, "would understand him."

Alongside this barbed element of the "sin issue," I began to discover that as well as highlighting my present state, it seemed that God's plan was not to leave me there but provide a remedy, a release. There was an awful lot of reading about "sin" and God's dealing with it. The general sense coming through was a certain helplessness in mankind, a condition from which there seemed to be no hope of liberation. I certainly didn't regard myself as "sinner" material, but something about this pricked my conscience and spoke to my condition, which was quite uncomfortable. I pressed on though because I was doing this for my friend.

The strange thing was that Derek had always talked to me about Jesus during our time together in Los Angeles. I knew all about Jesus because we'd studied him in school. But now, as I moved into the New Testament, the Jesus described there and the one that I thought I knew were apparently two completely different people.

Although, on the surface, nothing was moving me, but inside me was the question of "Why are we here?" and, as I read the Bible, it seemed to be telling me that I was here because God had a purpose in it.

But I couldn't reconcile myself to this God because of the world in which I lived. I also had always remembered a quote that we had heard in school when we had studied the Russian Revolution. It was by Karl Marx who had boldly declared, "religion is the opiate of the masses."

Coming from a working class family [in England], there was a certain appeal to the class struggle that took place in Russia and it was one of the few times that I was genuinely interested in something we studied at school. I guess, though, our British "class struggle" was rather predictable. Voting Labor was a matter of course, regardless of the candidate.

The more I read, the more I realized that the God whom I thought I knew as the God of Christianity was far removed from the God who was revealed in the pages of the Bible. I read about Jesus, I found myself on occasions really touched by His compassion and caring for ordinary people. He seemed to be for the common man and he definitely seemed to have a bee in his bonnet about suffocating, self-righteous, religious attitudes that oppressed rather than liberated.

In a few months, I got through the whole Bible with not too many answers to give Derek, but I'd certainly given myself a lot of food for my own personal thought.

After I put down my Bible, I muttered to myself, "What about all the other religions. Well, they're all the same, aren't they?"

To make sure that they were "all the same" I amassed an amazing assortment of books on any religion I could find and began to study them. I welcomed the approach of the people who hang out in airport terminals, donated to their cause and received with delight their books of enrichment and enlightenment, which made for strange reading. I think my friends on the road crew thought that I had smoked one joint too many and never came back.

It was actually funny, because here was this anti-Christian pseudo-intellectual pouring over books on Buddhism, Hare Krishna and Islam. You name it and I found it. And I kept catching myself saying, "Well, that's .all very well, but that's not what the Bible says." Which confused me all the more.

I came to one firm conclusion, and that was that all religions aren't the same; that the choices and opinions are endless. Most of them were a little too strange for even me. So much pressure to perform; to capture the attention of "God," whoever he might be. And there always seemed to be the threat that if I blew it in this life, I'd come back in the next as maybe an ant that somebody was going to step on, and that would be my just desserts for the life that I had led.

I came away from all of this with a line drawn in my heart knowing that there was a great difference between Christianity and all the other religions and a sense that this was a book that understood me, which was a little scary. That much I was prepared to concede. But where it fitted in with me I wasn't sure. I'd certainly come to an awareness that if God was real, there wasn't much I could do to impress him and, although I regarded myself as a pretty good person—after all, I'd never murdered anybody—His standard was different, unattainable apart from a relationship with Christ.

But Jesus and rock and roll didn't seem to form a strong relationship and rock and roll I knew; Jesus I wasn't too sure about.

I asked all of my friends on our bus their opinion of Christianity. We all pretty much agreed that it was absolutely certain that we were all Christians. We were English, basically good-natured with no plans to do any harm, just out to enjoy life and obviously worthy and destined to do well at the pearly gates! The best thing for me was to stop trying to be something I already was. Funnily enough though, the more we talked about it, the more it seemed that all of our opinions and prejudices were far removed from the brand of Christianity that I had discovered in the Bible.

We almost got into fistfights over the concept of a loving God who allowed suffering in the world. A big source of conflict was the day we discussed forgiveness and whether or not God would let people like Hitler into heaven if they were truly sorry for what they had done. That discussion got so heated that it startled our driver and our bus almost ran off the road as we yelled and screamed at each other. These were heady topics to discuss in the cramped confines of a tour bus full of tired and cranky roadies.

I found myself vehemently defending the Gospel, but not actually committed to it in a tangible way in my own life. But something had touched my heart and, for the first time in my life, the hard shell of anger and frustration that had encrusted my heart, was beginning to peel away.

I took our conversations seriously and began to ask questions of this God that I wasn't too sure that I believed in. I was just as confused about those issues as the other guys were, but I could not "buy" the argument that it was okay to do what you were doing until you got older and then, when you were too decrepit to have fun anymore, you then became a normal Christian, stop having fun, settle down and get married—the two went hand in hand— and go to church for Christmas and Easter. At least that seemed to be the general consensus. Something told me that there was more to it than that; that it was something that I needed to take a hold of now. That maybe waiting was a dangerous thing to do.

Perhaps it was the fact that I had already experienced the death of people around me that told me that there weren't guarantees that we were all going to live to a ripe old age.

But then what?

Barry then described the start of the AC/DC concert where his life was to change forever.

As the arena lights lowered, a full-throated anticipatory roar rose from the 18,000 hardcore AC/DC fans assembled at the Kobo Arena in Detroit.

That deafening wall of sound and the sight of a thousand points of flickering light emanating from cigarette lighters throughout the indoor arena was an amazing spectacle for me, even after I had witnessed so many concerts all over the world.

Cliff Williams, who was now the band's bass player, began the intro to AC/DC's standard opener, "Problem Child." As his bass thumped the opening rhythm, the crowd's roar rose to a crescendo. Phil then kicked in with his bass drum, quickly followed by the combined crunching power chords of Angus and Malcolm's guitars.

A solitary spotlight picked out Bon as he launched into a primeval scream, his trademark introduction. The lights onstage then came flashing on and lit up the arena and we were off into another night of uninhibited rock and roll.

My sole job now with the group was to set up Phil's drums, mix the sound for his monitor system, and generally take care of his needs. Phil Rudd, the AC/DC drummer, and I had become quite close friends and we roomed together. We had weathered a lot of situations in which I helped through periods of extreme stress on the road. He liked to be in close communication even during the concert, so I arranged the stage equipment so I could stand less than three feet away from him throughout the concert, mix the sound, and yet not be seen by anyone.

We had been on the road for a few months, so there were few problems. Everything had settled into a well-oiled routine and was running smoothly. This was a good concert with an excited audience. It's amazing how an audience can affect the way a band plays. If the electricity is there from them that seemed to draw out the best in the band, if not a show can often go flat.

Of course, I'd heard these AC/DC songs year after year and knew every chord change and pretty much everything that would happen in the concert. They would play favorites from albums like "High Voltage," "Let There Be Rock," "Powerage," "If You Want Blood, You've Got it" and "Highway to Hell."

Barry then recalled what happened during that concert:

Here I was in the middle of this concert and a thought flashed through my head: "Barry, you've either got to forget all this God stuff and carry on with the life you're living, or stop it all and go on with God."

I could sense the emotions lying just beneath the surface like a volcano about to erupt and, as the music receded into the background of my awareness, I reflected on the life I had been living. I came to the conclusion that I didn't particularly want to carry on in that way. In my mind's eye, I scanned the past few years of my existence and came to the conclusion that all I had done in my efforts to find answers and some kind of Inner peace, had resulted in me becoming a hard-hearted, cynical, drug-wasted, young man. Outwardly I was not a bad person, in fact I was generally congenial and easy to get on with, but inside was locked away a desperate person, troubled and unsettled.

The future of continuing in that life seemed quite bleak. Everything was tolerable, in fact, more than that, provided I didn't examine it too closely. All at once I felt an overwhelming sense of futility and loneliness. Flocked images tumbled over one another in my mind. The one thing that I had discovered was that for all their Initial pleasures, drugs had not been that good to me. It had become more of a chore than an enjoyment now, a habit, the routine of buying, taking, getting high then coming down. My body had become wasted and I had had some close brushes with what I can only believe was death. Recently, every few months, I was having strange symptoms, almost like epileptic fits where I would lose control of my limbs and wind up shaking on the ground.

I also seemed to have a permanent cold, probably because of all the drugs I had put up my nose. My stomach was always upset, too. To maker matters worse I was regularly coughing up blood and had a hard time eating my food.

As much as I loved music, I realized there was no redemption in it, that my heroes, the musicians of my day, the people that our generation revered and worshiped, didn't have any answers either. They were ordinary people, who had an extraordinary occupation and lifestyle, but they were no different to anyone else. It was that brief moment each day when they strapped on their guitars and hit the stage that their lives had anything different going on in it. We value and prize fame, but it Is a strange and momentary phenomenon.

I had met a lot of great people, but no one seemed to have much of an idea of where we were going. I saw the folly of riches, the incredible lengths that people go to make it to the top and then the fickleness of humanity that leaves them next year for some other hero.

The band would sing once in a while, "It's a long way to the top if you want to rock and roll." It was a true statement. The whole concept of overnight success is, I think, the figment of some journalist's imagination. Quite honestly, I wondered if making it to the top had any point to it anyway. It didn't for Janis Joplin and Jimmy Hendrix.

I had rejected most of the standards of my, day. I regarded them as shallow and hypocritical and I had developed my new morality, which was do your own thing and screw everybody else—as politely as possible, of course, but I was just as shallow and hypocritical.

Then there was all this God stuff.

I had to come to terms with the fact that I wasn't a Christian. I may have been exposed to certain Christian ethics, but what the Bible had to say about being a Christian was far removed from what I was. And even though I still had a lot of unanswered questions, I had pretty much accepted that perhaps a lot of the problems in the world that God got ultimate blame for were born out of the fact that generally God wasn't invited into the situations in the first place. I'm not sure that I could lay the blame for people starving to death In India on God because I didn't see Him inviting them to worship rats, which spread disease and allowing cows to be regarded as holy animals who had the right to roam around and eat whatever they liked while people starved to death.

In some ways, I think I had anger at God even though outwardly I claimed no belief In Him. Maybe I was mad that I'd been born into this generation, living in a council house, flung into a world full of potential nuclear disaster, human injustice and all the rest of the stuff that plagues our world. And then, there was Jesus Christ who supposedly came to reveal who God was to this world.

A friend of mine had once said in a discussion that the thing that bothered him about Christianity was that it was too simple. But maybe that was the point. We live in such a complex world that it would appear that we feel we need incredibly complicated answers. But from what I'd read, I had to concede that the God of the Bible seemed to have a firm grasp on the reality of the human condition and, on that basis, He had provided an answer that He himself would come and live as a man in this world and take upon Himself all of the sins, the ugliness of this world.

In that moment, as the band played on, I became really aware of who Barry Taylor was at that moment in time, the hypocrisies, the absolute emptiness of my life.

"I don't want to carry on this way," I finally resolved, marshalling all my strength.

So really, for me at that moment, there was no choice. I realized the beckoning of a God who even when we don't believe in Him, is at work. Who even when we deny His existence, has a plan and a purpose for us being on the planet and who, in His great love, sent his son to save us from ourselves.

I knew that I was going to choose to give my life to God. I wasn't sure what that meant—Billy Graham wasn't there to tell me what to do and how to do it! And so, with that resolution firmly set in my heart, I prayed for the first time, "God, please get this concert over quickly so I can give my life to You!"

I suppose that I could have made the commitment right there and then but, for some reason I decided to wait until after the show, and do it on the tour bus.

The concert didn't end any quicker, but once it was over, I worked like a man possessed, harder than I had in a long time, dismantling the equipment and carrying it outside. Once we had got all the trucks loaded, I ran onto the bus for our short journey to Chicago. There's not a great distance between these two great cities, and so we had picked up a few extra passengers. By the time our bus pulled onto the freeway, a rip-roaring party was already in full swing.

The bus's stereo system was blasting rock and roll—the porno video that we'd all seen time and time again was running once more on a television set up close to the front of the bus -- drinks were flowing—drugs were being consumed and a "good time" was being had by all, except by me.

In the midst of all of this I took out my Bible. I wasn't sure how I was supposed to do this. I flipped through it but that didn't seem to be making much sense. I tried to remember some prayers that we had prayed at school in our morning assemblies, and one that sprang to mind was something that our headmaster recited quite often. It said, "Teach us good Lord, to serve thee as thou deserveth, to give and not to count the cost, to fight and not to heed the wounds, to toil and not to seek for rest, to labor and not to seek for any reward save that of knowing that we do Thy will." My vigil of waiting was over and radiance lit up my usually pale face.

How I remembered that, I don't know. But somehow that night when I said it, I wasn't going through the motions as when I'd been at school making jokes and cracking up with my friends and eye-ing the girls. But it was with all my heart. I really meant it and so, after that, I said, "God, I want the life that you have for me. Whatever it is and whatever it takes, I want to live for you in the earth. Amen!"

What came next, I wasn't sure. But I was sure that something was going to have to change—and soon.

Barry then told me that soon that change came about and he left AC/DC and moved to Los Angeles where Derek "discipled him" with a deep grounding in scripture and lessons on what it meant to follow Christ. This eventually resulted in Barry finally making a career change was had been unthinkable a few months before—he began helping out at Lake Arrowhead Christian Fellowship and then becoming its senior pastor.

Our friendship blossomed, and Barry would pay a weekly visit to me in Orange County, where Norma I now lived, so we could have lunch together and share what was happening in our lives.

After a couple of years, I began to feel that it was time for Norma and I to move on from Open Doors and possibly start a new min-istry. "Barry, I'd like to do more than just write and broadcast about the persecuted church, but I am not sure how to do this," I told him one day.

Barry began to suggest that I started a new ministry that possi-bly could be linked with his church in the mountains and this finally turned into what is now called ASSIST Ministries.

He then surprised me when he said, "Dan, if you ever get a chance for me to go to Russia to do some work there, I'd love to go because I speak fluent Russian."

I paused for a moment, thinking he was joking. "But," I protest-ed, "Roadies can hardly speak English, let alone Russian. How come you speak Russian?"

Seeing my disbelief, he told me that after he had been discipled by Derek in Los Angeles, he felt God was telling him to take an intensive course in the Russian language, which he did. He also said that he could speak several languages including French, German and Dutch.

I filed away his request and began to ask my friends to come up with a name for our new group. Geoff Booker, a friend from England, who was over visiting Barry's church, brainstormed with me and finally said, as we drove down the road from the mountain-top into San Bernardino, "I've got it. You should call it ASSIST." We played around with the acronym and I came up with Aid to Suffering Saints in Serious Trouble to fit with ASSIST."

One day I was sharing my vision to start a new organization with Dr. Dale Kietzman, the former U.S. director of Wycliffe Bible Translators and the man, who when he was with Open Doors, had sponsored our move to the United States. He warmed to the idea, helped us with our non-profit papers and soon we were in business. Barry joined with Dale and other friends to join our board of directors.

Jackie Yockey, the guest coordinator for the 700 Club heard about ASSIST and invited me to launch it on the show. I flew to Virginia Beach and we did just that with Sheila Walsh as the host.

After the show was broadcast, I was inundated with phone calls from friends saying that the acronym Aid to Suffering Saints in Serious Trouble was terrible. "Dan," one said, "They are not suffering saints but are victorious saints and they are not in serious trouble; we in the West are the ones in serious trouble with our emphasis on money and fame."

After prayer, I changed it to Aid to Special Saints in Strategic Times!

Norma and I made our first ASSIST trip overseas to Havana, Cuba, with David Tamez, a Mexican Christian who knew the believers of the island very well. We then launched a Sister Church program, which linked U.S. churches with Cuban congregations. It has continued for years now and one of the churches now supports 250 or so pastors in Cuba on a monthly basis.

Meeting these beautiful Cuban Christians was such a great experience to us both, but definitely different to what happened on another trip to Bethlehem, the birthplace of Jesus.

I had initially agreed to go to Jerusalem in December 2000 to report on "Celebrate Messiah," the final event of the AD2000 & Beyond Movement. But then came the news that the immigration department of Israel was on strike and many of the delegates from the Developing World could not get visas to travel to Jerusalem, so the event was cancelled.

"How would you like to go to Israel with me?" I asked Norma who had never been there before. "I have a non-refundable ticket and so I could change the travel dates and get you a ticket as well."

Bethlehem was to be the highlight of the visit for us as it was not only the birthplace of Jesus Christ, but also I wanted her to see the Bethlehem Bible College. I had previously stayed in Bethlehem for five days some three years earlier as part of a team that went there to celebrate Brother Andrew's 70th birthday. This intrepid Dutchman, who authored his best-selling book, *God's Smuggler*, was a wonderful host and showed us around the historic town and even took us into Hebron during a gun battle between the Israeli forces and the Palestinians.

As the sound of gunfire echoed around Hebron, I interviewed Brother Andrew, asking him, "Why should we love Muslims?"

A slight smile crept into his face and the then said, "Because I believe that ISLAM should stand for I Sincerely Love All Muslims." In a later interview, he told me, "You will never win a Muslim to Christ unless you show that person that you are not afraid to die."

On that gloomy Middle Eastern day, we had not idea that we were about to face death. Outside the St. George's Cathedral Guest House where we were staying in East Jerusalem, we found an Arab taxi driver that agreed to take us into the ancient city, but when we arrived at the Israeli checkpoint, we found that the Israelis had sealed off the city because it was the Orthodox Christmas Day and many religious leaders as well as Yasser Arafat where to attend a special service at the Church of the Nativity, which marks the birthplace of Jesus.

"I know a back way into Bethlehem," the driver told us as he smiled knowingly, and soon we were entering Bethlehem through new route. It was a strange feeling as there were many trucks ahead of us winding their way through what seemed to be a stone quarry. As soon as we arrived, I noticed gunmen everywhere. As we got close to the Church of the Nativity, five young gunmen, who we were later told were possibly from the Islamic Jihad, stopped our vehicle. They saw the yellow Israeli plates on the car, and they began shouting as they surrounded the taxi and it became extremely ugly.

Our taxi driver, whose face drained and had turned white, kept shouting to them in Arabic that he was "an Arab" and we were

"Americans." We silently prayed in the back of the vehicle and after about three heart-stopping minutes, the gunmen suddenly backed off and an older man, who appeared to be their leader, banged on to top of the taxi, and waved us through.

We thanked the driver for saving our lives and, as he recovered his composure, he told us, "They thought you were Jewish Settlers and were going to pull you out of the taxi and shoot you both."

Our hearts stood still for a moment as we realized how close we had come to death. I finally gathered my composure and told Norma, "Maybe the Lord still has some work for us to do."

Soon we were at Manger Square and we entered the almost empty church and went to the top of the stairway where a star had been placed to mark what many believe was the actual spot of His birth. There we paused to thank the Lord for his watch-care over us.

The phone rang in my office and I picked up the receiver to discover that it was Stuart Bennett on the line. Stuart had worked as a film editor for BBC TV at the Ealing Studios when I had lived in the area and also had worked on a film directed by Tony Tew, who was part of our "Road Block to Moscow" team. The film was called "Greenbelt Live," and was about the famous Christian arts and music festival in England that that year starred Cliff Richard and Randy Stonehill, Lamb and Larry Norman.

"Dan, I've just moved to Virginia Beach to work for CBN and they have asked me to produce a TV show called, 'What Are You Living For?' for Soviet State TV. It will be a fast-moving MTV-style program which will present the gospel to the youth of the Soviet Union.

"I've got a band called No Longer Music to perform in it, also a Russian lady to be a host but I need a Western co-host that speaks fluent Russian and would appeal to the kids there. Do you know of anyone who fits that description?"

I paused for a moment and then said, "Well, I have a suggestion." I told him about Barry Taylor and said that he had told me that he spoke fluent Russian and I added, "He certainly would appeal to the youth of the Soviet Union. He used to be with AC/DC."

I could sense the shock at my recommendation but Stuart went ahead and contacted Barry and arranged for him to have a Russian-language test over the phone. He passed with flying colors and was hired to be the Western co-host for the show.

Barry was actually flying into Moscow to start taping the program when on August 18, 1991, Soviet leader, Mikhail Gorbachev and his family, were placed under house arrest at their vacation home in Crimea. A coup attempt that briefly ousted Gorbachev had begun in Moscow.

On August 19, 1991, the coup leaders, including hardliners in the Communist Party, the Soviet Army and the KGB, declared a state of emergency and sent tanks into Moscow. Russia's President Boris Yeltsin led tens of thousands in resisting the coup. After demonstrations in Moscow that involved at least three deaths, the coup collapsed August 21, eventually dragging the Soviet Union down with it.

When Barry arrived and was told of what had occurred, he suggested that they take a camera crew to the Russian White house where tens of thousands of Russians had gathered and he asked them what they were living for? Most of them said it was for "drugs, sex and rock and roll." It was an unusual start to the making of the program.

As they began taping the segments in which footage of AC/DC was included, three senior officials implicated in the failed coup committed suicide and more than a dozen others were arrested. The treason trial of the coup plotters, who called themselves the Emergency Situation Committee, started in April 1993, but the case was repeatedly postponed because of poor health of the defendants and procedural problems.

The trial was eventually suspended indefinitely in May 1994. The defendants were granted amnesty by Russia's new lower house of parliament, the State Duma. The amnesty also freed top officials who led the October 1993 parliamentary-Supreme Soviet-rebellion.

As things settled down in Moscow, Barry for the final segment of the show stood by the side of the Moscow River and gave an invitation to camera for people watching to give their lives over to Jesus Christ, just as he had done outside that area in Detroit. The contact addresses of where people could write were flashed on the screen at the end of the program and Barry returned home.

"Dan," said Stuart's voice on the end of the phone line, "you won't believe the response we have received from the TV show. Millions of young people have written in to us telling us they have given their lives to Christ. We can hardly cope with the letters that keep pouring in."

Later, Stuart suggested that we might like to start a pen pal program linking these new Soviet believers with Christian friends in the West. This was the beginning of our Bridge of Friendship program and soon we were handling letters at our Garden Grove office from 76,000 of these new converts and we began to link them. The project continues today, but we have also expanded it to include new friends in China and Taiwan.

And it all began with a meeting with the former roadie of AC/DC.

By the way, Barry is now completing a Ph.D. course in Post Modern Studies at the School of World Missions at Fuller Theological Seminary in Pasadena, California; teaches a course there in popular culture, has recorded several music CDs of his own music and leads a church for people in the media and the entertainment industry in Southern California.

25
A Miracle In Moscow

As ASSIST was beginning to grow, I had all but abandoned my day-to-day journalism work. I had lingering shame about my tabloid career in London's Fleet Street, and so I concentrated on running the ministry. After all, wasn't that more spiritual?

But that changed when I received a phone call from Larry Ross, Billy Graham's press officer, in July of 1991.

"Dan, you know that Mr. Graham has been going to Russia for years now," said Larry.

"Yes, and we are running a pen pal ministry there with new believers," I cut in thinking that he wanted to know more about the ASSIST Russia "Bridge of Friendship" program.

Larry said he thought that was "very interesting" and then added, "Mr. Graham has been invited to Moscow to hold a crusade there. It will be the first time that he can openly invite people to receive Christ."

He paused for a moment, and then said, "We'd like you to come and join our media team and use your journalistic skills to report on this historic Mission to Moscow."

I felt all the air being sucked out of my lungs when he then said, "We feel your tabloid skills could be used to portray what is going to happen there. When could you get on a plane to Moscow?"

I stammered my thanks and said that I would be honored to go and so he said arrangements would be made for my air ticket and visa and he would like me there as soon as possible.

When I put the receiver down, Norma looked at me in a strange way. "What's up?" she asked. "You have gone as pale as milk."

"Larry wants me to fly to Moscow to join his media team and use my journalistic skills," I said trying to take in what was being asked of me. After all, I had once worked for Mr. Graham on *The Christian* and after losing my job I never dreamed I would ever be able to work with him again.

From Tabloid To Truth

I recalled how one day, someone had told me that I really couldn't write and I believed that. I had figured that my tabloid past had been a complete waste of time and could not be used by the Lord.

Norma smiled and said pointedly, "It's a good job that Billy Graham doesn't know that you can write...."

Within a few days, the tickets and the visa had come through and I drove to Los Angeles International Airport to fly to Moscow, via Frankfurt, Germany.

Before I left, I had sent a message to Alexander Ogorodnikov, a Christian dissident who had spent many years in the Gulag for his faith—and for running a Christian discussion group at the Moscow State University, where he had found salvation after viewing a film about the Life of Christ.

Alexander was eventually sent to Perm 36, one of the worst prisons in the Soviet Union where quite a number of famous prisoners were kept, including Anatoly Schiransky, Alexander went on many hunger strikes. The guards would take his Bible and Orthodox Cross, which he wore around his neck, from him and so he would then refuse to eat. He would say, "I would rather die than be without the Word of God."

After five years of this terrible existence, Alexander finally cracked and wrote a letter to his mother which was heart wrenching. In it he wrote,

> Therefore, I repeat request, a decision I reached after much thought and suffering. You must see that death appears to be the only way to end my agony, the only release, I have already committed the grave sin of attempting to commit suicide: on the 1st, 9th and 17th of May 1984 I secretly cut my veins, but every time I was discovered, unconscious but still alive, so they gave me blood transfusions. So I beg of you again—please appeal to the Presidium of the Supreme Soviet to show me a measure of mercy by ordering my execution by firing squad in order to put an end to the prospect of lifelong, painfully slow torture by deprivation of living conditions fit for a human being, deprivations of books, culture, torture by hunger, cold, by incarceration in punishment cells, humiliations, total lack of rights.... They even forbid me to pray, and my cross has been torn from around my neck on numerous occasions. I have spent a total of 659 days on hunger strike to protest against their refusal to let me have a Bible and a prayer-book, and 411 days in the internal camp prison.... I do not know whether there

was one Christian anywhere who expressed support for me during those 659 days of hunger strike, and it frightens me to think that maybe there wasn't.

I received an English translation of Alexander's anguished message from Keston College I in England, a center for the study of religion under communism. I was saddened when I first read his letter, feeling that we in the West had so let him down by not supporting him.

I managed to get the mailing address of the labor camp where he was being held and went on national television in the United States and asked Christians to not only pray for Alexander, but also bombard the camp with messages of support.

Apparently, Margaret Thatcher, then the Prime Minister of Great Britain, heard of his case and during a visit to Moscow, asked Mr. Gorbachev to free him. Amazingly, he agreed to the "Iron Lady's" request and so I was anxious to meet him in Moscow, where he was now running a home for battered women and children.

After checking into the President Hotel, a secret place that had been built for communist leaders visiting Moscow like Kim Il Sung, I went to bed to get a good night's sleep.

The next morning, I received a call from the front desk saying, "a man called Alexander is here and wants to see you."

I rushed down the stairs and there was Alexander, dressed in a pinstriped suit, wearing granny glasses and with a ponytail hairstyle. He was nothing like I had imagined.

"Dan," he said extending his hand to me. "Thank you for caring!" I had to choke back the tears as he said this.

I then took him into the restaurant for breakfast where Larry Ross and some of the Billy Graham team members joined us.

There, after the coffee was poured, he turned to me and asked me to tell him more about how I had got Christians to write to him.

"Did you ever see the letters?" I asked him.

"Yes, they would take me into a room filled with sacks of mail, but would not let me read any of them," he began. "But I can't describe my feeling when I realized that people did care after all."

He then locked his eyes on mine and asked, "Did you ask people to pray for me?"

I nodded.

"I thought so," he continued after taking a sip from his coffee cup. "Let me tell you what happened. After they would show me the sacks of mail from America, they would take me to a punishment cell where they hoped I would die from the cold. I would just have flimsy clothes on and the cell was like a block of ice. I would begin to shiver and soon hypothermia would set in and I knew that I didn't have long to live.

"Then a miracle would happen. I believe that God would wake up someone who saw you on television there in America and they would begin to pray for me and suddenly I felt God's arms around me like a comforter and warmth would flow back into my freezing body. This happened several times and again I want to say, 'Thank you for caring.'"

After an extended breakfast, we parted company, and I just wanted to cry with joy that this amazing man of faith had been delivered from the Gulag and who had wanted to say "Thank you" for what had happened.

Shortly after that, I was asked to lead the devotions for some of the Graham team. I spoke about the man with the withered hand who had been healed by Jesus. "I believe that many of the Russian people have had their faith withered away through communism and now Mr. Graham has been chosen of God to help heal the nation with his message of love and joy and many will no longer have a 'withered faith' but will instead have a personal relationship with the great healer—Jesus Christ."

It wasn't long before Larry Ross introduced me to Billy Graham, who remembered the days of *The Christian*. I was taken aback with his humbleness and soon began to realize that this was the key to the way God has used him over the years. He knew he could trust fame with a man like this who always remembered his simple roots as he grew up on a farm outside of Charlotte, North Carolina.

Early on, Mr. Graham was asked to deliver a sermon at the Moscow Baptist Church and I joined the overflow crowds in that historic church. He then addressed a press conference and was asked by one journalist, "Mr. Graham, did you not realize that when you would speak at the Moscow Baptist Church in the past, the authorities would clear out the front few pews and fill them with KGB officers. What do you say to that?"

Mr. Graham paused, smiled quietly and then replied, "Well,

that's good news. After all, they more than most needed to hear the Gospel."

The first of the three nights of the crusade began in the huge indoor Olympic Stadium. It was quite ironic since here was an American preaching at a venue where Jimmy Carter had forbade the U.S. Olympic team to participate in the Moscow Olympics as a protest against the Soviet invasion of Afghanistan.

As Cliff Barrows led the huge Russian choir in the singing of "How Great Though Art," I noticed a dove-liked bird fly from where the choir was located and flutter around the arena. It was quite symbolic to a tabloid hack like myself. The Holy Spirit was descending on the crusade as a sign of what was to come.

The second night was for the Russian military and I watched thousands of men dressed in Russian military uniforms file in and take their places in seats around the stadium. Then, I got my video camera ready as the Red Army Choir began singing, "The Battle Hymn of the Republic." Their magnificent voices rose as they sang, "Glory, Glory, Hallelujah, His truth is marching on."

I felt goose bumps rise in my arms as I tried to steady the camera. After all, this was the propaganda choir of the former Soviet Union singing the truth of the Gospel.

I then went back to the press table and watched as Mr. Graham approached the podium and preached for an hour. He then gave the invitation and suddenly we were greeted with a loud cacophony of marching boots on the cement floor of the stadium. Soldiers, sailors and airmen began running to the front to receive Christ.

As he watched the race to the front, a startled Billy Graham tried to explain what it meant to make a commitment to Christ thinking that many had misunderstood his call to commitment. But they just kept running until almost the entire huge space in front of the platform was full of military men and some women, many kneeling.

Soon, Mr. Graham was leading this sea of people in the "Sinner's Prayer," and even the hardest of journalists covering the event were close to tears. Who would have believed that so many of our former enemies were now brothers and sisters in Christ?

Before the final meeting, a group of us went to the Lubyanka, the former headquarters of the KGB, a place where many Christians were said to have been tortured to death. During the days of communism, it was a crime to photograph this infamous building.

When we arrived at the Lubyanka, I noticed that a statue of the founder of the KGB had been toppled and a banner had been strung across the statue. Not understanding Russian, I asked someone in the crowd what the slogan said.

He said, "It says, 'The Cross is Victorious.'"

We then headed for the Olympic Stadium and it took us quite a while to work our way through the crowds—60,000 were inside and thousands were sitting and standing in the cold watching the proceedings on a big-screen television.

As I made my way to the press table, I noticed about 500 people sitting in wheelchairs and amongst them I saw Joni Eareckson-Tada, the American quadriplegic. Soon, Joni was wheeled to the side of the stage, lifted up and began to give her testimony. Igor, a blind man who stood by her, was interpreting her.

Then it was Mr. Graham's turn and he preached an incredible sermon. Everyone was quiet as he spoke in English and was interpreted by Vicktor Hamm. When he gave the invitation, people began streaming out from their seats and just kept on coming.

I was standing next to an American pastor who wept like a baby as he saw what was happening. "Who would have believed that so many of the Russian people would give their lives to Christ?" he said.

Then he added, "Do you know what has happened here tonight?"

Before I could reply, he said, "God used a cripple, a blind man and a 74-year-old man with Parkinson's disease to reach Russia with the Gospel."

27
The Bride Who Preached
At Her Wedding

After traveling the world now for 30 years as a journalist, I thought I'd just about seen everything. But then I met Sister Esther, a diminutive and dynamic Chinese Christian, and she topped my previous experiences.

The surprise took place during a recent visit to China when Norma and I attended Esther's wedding to a Christian man. The ceremony was held in an official church in a city I cannot name.

After the moving ceremony, in which I briefly participated as an ordained minister from America, Esther took over the microphone and, in her white wedding dress, began preaching to the packed congregation. During her 30-minute sermon, she didn't pull any punches. She told the people assembled, many of whom were not Christians, that they needed to "believe in Jesus."

Then, in a moving moment, she asked her mother, once a committed Communist, to step forward. As the congregation watched in hushed silence, she then led her mother in a public "sinner's prayer."

Esther later told me, "I became a Christian when I was 13 years old, after walking by a Christian church. The first time I came in contact with Christianity I knew it was true. I was so thrilled to hear about Jesus Christ that I knew I had to follow Him." Later she listened to Christian radio coming from Hong Kong to strengthen her faith.

Her conversion caused her great anguish, as her father was a local Communist cadre who was considered in his city to be a hero because he had fought against the Japanese during World War II and in the Chinese civil war for Chairman Mao. "Both of my parents were shocked with the news and told me that they did not approve, as this had caused them to lose face."

She said, "One night, my father scolded me very hard and I got so depressed. I just cried for hours. But then the Holy Spirit told me, 'You are God's child and you are upset because you have allowed the devil to work in your life. Do you believe in the devil or in Jesus?' I said I believed in Jesus. Then the Holy Spirit made me think of the story of Job. I then said, 'My Lord, I love you and want to serve only You.' The Holy Spirit then revealed to me that if I wanted to win people to Christ, I must suffer persecution."

The persecution did continue for Esther. "Whenever I would come in from church, my parents would be very angry with me and scold me very hard," she said.

"After many years of this, I asked Jesus, 'Lord, why is my life so hard? I think maybe you don't love me."

She said the answer came one day when she rode her bicycle to work. "When I reached a bridge in my town, I felt God telling me, 'If you want to be like a doctor and help people, you first have to understand what it is to be hurt.' He then prompted me to begin reading 1 Corinthians 13. I then realized what it means to love people. I knew that I had to understand people's hurts to be able to help them. I told the Lord, 'I'm very happy, because I know that you love me.'"

She added, "I am also now very happy to be a Bride of Christ so I can work for Jesus among my people."

Esther explained that in those days, her parents did not have a happy marriage and she had to share a bed with her mother. "I know my mother did not like me being a believer and so I would wait for her to go to sleep and then I would pull the covers over my face and turn on my radio and listen quietly to the Christian broadcasts coming from Hong Kong, the receiver pressed close to my ear. It was like having a Bible School coming to me and I was greatly built up in my faith because of these broadcasts."

Soon, Esther, despite being threatened with losing her job, began openly witnessing to her colleagues at work and teaching the Bible at a local church. She also began wearing a cross around her neck as a public confession of her faith. (She still wears it today.)

Her father has since passed away. "Before he died, I was able to lead him to Christ. Then I led my mother to a faith in the Lord. Their marriage was restored and their marriage went from a Communist marriage to a Christian marriage. After they became Christians, they really began to love each other," she said.

"Before I got married, I asked my mother if she would be will-ing to make a public confession at my wedding in front of everyone who knew her. She agreed and that is why she prayed publicly with me after the wedding ceremony. It was a wonderful occasion for me."

Women, as Norma and I soon discovered on this visit, play a leading role in the Chinese church. Many women bring their husbands to walk two hours to church each Sunday then, after the service, walk another two hour back home. "They do it because they love Jesus and also want to be with other believers," Esther explained.

She continued, "When I think of the courage and faith of my Chinese brothers and sisters, I want to cry. They are so committed to Jesus. I think they are the best brothers and sisters in the world."

Esther revealed that the government has decreed that no one under eighteen years of age can be taught the Bible, but that doesn't make any difference to her. "I teach a weekly Sunday School class," she said.

"I still listen to Christian radio and I take notes and the Holy Spirit teaches me God's truths," she said. "I know that, in America, you have many wonderful Bible teachers, but I want you to know that I believe the best teacher is the world is the Holy Spirit."

I told Esther that I had heard that there had been a great revival in China, possibly now with up to 80 million believers there. "In the countryside around where I live, some 90 percent of the people are believers," she said. "Many miracles take place in the countryside and there are healings there after people pray.

"However, so much of the population lives in the city and so many of the young people there are not being reached for the Lord. This is why I am so fervent in sharing the Gospel with them. If a young person goes to church in China, they are looked down upon. So few people go to the official church and they are usually only the older people. So we have to reach the city youth of China."

She said that the countryside Christians mainly attend House Churches, also known as Family Churches. "They are very committed and pray for hours everyday and, if they can get a Bible, they study it. Those who can't get Bibles, often listen to Christian radio and copy down the Bible by hand as it is read over the air.

During our visit to China, Esther and her new husband acted

as hosts for us. I got a real insight into her heart for the Lord when we met with students at a university to share with them that we wanted to find friends in America for them to correspond with through the ASSIST Bridge of Friendship China program. We had lunch with them on the campus and she asked them if they would all join hands so she could bless the food. She then prayed, "Lord, I ask You that these students may learn the truth about You."

As a footnote to this story, I discovered that, after Norma and I had left the city were the wedding took place, the senior pastor of the official church was summoned by the local communist authorities who had discovered that I, as a foreigner, had taken part in the wedding. He was severely censored for allowing me to do this. This news vividly illustrated to me that China still does not have the religious freedom it claims!

Sister Esther is now living in America with his husband, but she is broadcasting the Gospel back to her home country and helping us with our Bridge of Friendship China e-pal program. The Bridge of Friendship is a unique way anyone can become a friend with someone in countries like China, Taiwan and Russia. This ASSIST program, which is explained in detail on the ASSIST website, has linked thousands of Western Christians with believers and non-believers in these countries. It is a wonderful way to bridge misunderstanding and promote friendship between people from totally different backgrounds.

27
Tears In Heaven For Jeff

Jeff, a 16-year-old Brazilian illegal immigrant to the United States was just skin and bone as he lay in his bed. He had full-blown AIDS and like thousands of other hemophiliacs, had contracted the deadly virus from tainted blood products.

As I stood at his bedside I felt helpless. Alongside of me was Mike Hylton, a father of three teenagers, who also was an HIV-positive hemophiliac. Next to him was Herb Hall, a tall imposing looking young man who had AIDS.

After a few moments of awkward silence Herb finally looked at this very ill young man and said, "Jeff, we would like to tell you about Jesus Christ and His love for you."

Jeff looked sadly at us and said, "Thank you, but I don't want to hear this from you. I am a Jehovah Witness. When I was hurting the Jehovah Witnesses were the only people who came to me when I first became sick. I've now joined their church."

Then he fixed his dull eyes at us and asked us, "Where were you Christians at that time?"

We were silent because we knew that some of what he said was sadly true. Much of the Church in America and around the world had turned their backs on those with HIV/AIDS and many had cruelly judged them. It was common at that time to hear people saying, "AIDS is God's judgment on the Gay community" or "you've got what you deserve."

For about an hour we tried to explain to Jeff the difference between the Jesus of the Jehovah Witnesses and the Jesus of the Bible but he just couldn't see it. We soon just made small talk with this emaciated young man as his mother watched, tears pouring down her cheeks. She knew she would soon lose her only son because she had not been able to seek help from the local authorities because of their illegal status.

Finally, with a feeling of helplessness, we said goodbye to Jeff. A few weeks later, Herb brought me the sad news that Jeff had passed away. That day I felt constrained to sit down and write about that heartbreaking experience. I called that article "Tears in Heaven for Jeff." I talked about our meeting with him and how he didn't want to hear about Jesus because he felt that Christians were not there for him in his his time of need.

It was a turning point in my life. I realized that this story couldn't end in defeat. There must be a better answer for the thousands and millions of "Jeff's" around the world. Soon I started work on a new book, a book of life and hope for those with HIV and AIDS, a book of people who knew that only Jesus, the real Jesus can give hope.

That book was to be called, *He Intends Victory*. He... Intends... Victory... It makes sense doesn't it? Jesus does intend victory even for those with HIV and AIDS. This book told the stories of people like Herb and Mike and how they had also at times felt rejected by the some Christians but because of the love of Christ had come to realize that it is not the Church that gives life but Jesus. They soon understood that the Church needed to be educated and that by putting a "face" on AIDS, maybe, just maybe, ignorant hearts and minds would change.

It wasn't long before the Lord led them to a small community of Christians at a church called The Village Church of Irvine. This small evangelical church had begun a ministry called "He Intends Victory" (HIV) to reach out to those infected and affected with the HIV virus that was fast becoming a pandemic around the world.

The connection with this small community had begun when I had received a phone call from a former Canadian grid iron footballer and former night club singer called Peter Turko, who had been working as a missionary in Uganda and had discovered another "holocaust" that was sweeping through the East African country. He said that Uganda, like many other countries in Africa, was experiencing a health epidemic that is being compared to the "bubonic plague. It was called AIDS."

"AIDS is taking a terrible toll on the people of Africa," said Turko, who runs "God's Love Ministries" and had been working in Uganda since 1986. "The disease is spreading at such a frightening rate that, if it is left unchecked, it could devastate an entire continent."

Turko pointed at the time to the statistics of millions of children orphaned throughout Africa by the AIDS epidemic and now hundreds of thousands of them were living on the streets. In the

Rakai district of Uganda alone, the disease has made orphans of one third of the children.

"Another 30 million more orphans in Africa are expected in the next ten years because of the deaths of their parents from AIDS," he said. "We have to act to help these children and adults who are dying without dignity in such terrible conditions."

Turko added during his phone call that that there were 5,500 funerals each day for AIDS victims in Africa and already 14 million had died. "Ten of the 22 million Africans infected with HIV can't afford even the cheapest medicines," he stated.

He then asked, "Dan, could you find me someone who understands AIDS and can advise me on what to do?"

I told him that I would make some inquires and then get back to him. Shortly after his call, I was listening to the "Tim and Al Show" on KBRT, a Southern California Christian radio station when their guest that day, Herb Hall, shared how he had discovered that he had AIDS after giving his life back to Christ after living in a homosexual life for ten years.

"I stood before my church congregation in Garden Grove, and confessed my sins," he said. "I had gone into the gay lifestyle and realized that what I had been doing was wrong and sinful. I soon gave my life back to Christ, fell in love with a young lady and wanted to propose marriage to her. However, because I had been in such a high-risk lifestyle, I thought I should be tested for HIV. To my shock I found out that I not only had HIV, but full-blown AIDS. My life seemed to fall apart. But I realized that there was only one place to turn. I turned to Jesus."

Herb said that prayer and counseling had begun to help him and he looked around for a support group, but could only find those for gay men. Finally, a friend told him about a new group that had started at the Village Church of Irvine, and so he began to attend and found a "sanctuary" with the people there.

Herb said that the pastor, Bruce Sonnenberg, had one Sunday morning asked his congregation if they believed that the church was meant to be a "hospital" where the sick could come to find help and healing by the love of Jesus, or just a "country club" where the members could sit back and hide from the world.

Pastor Sonnenberg said that he believed that God wanted this church to be a "hospital" where anyone could come, even those who were HIV-positive. He then asked that if they agreed, would they make a "stand" with him? Would they literally stand up and be counted? Slowly, agonizingly slowly at first, one by one, people stood up to where everyone in the church that morning stood up and a new ministry was birthed.

I managed to track down Herb after I heard that interview and he agreed to meet with Peter Turko and myself for lunch. Over the first of many wonderful meals together, Herb shared his story with us. When he finished, I said, "Herb, could I write up your story for a book?"

He paused for a long moment and then replied, "Dan, why don't you write a book about not only myself, but all my friends who have HIV/AIDS?"

Soon, Herb had taken me to see Bruce Sonnenberg and then Mike Hylton and slowly we began to put their stories down and soon we had the first edition of the book ready to go. Sheila Walsh, the talented and popular Scottish Christian singer and former co-host of the 700 Club, wrote a wonderful foreword for the book and it was published.

We agreed to launch it at the National Religious Broadcasters Convention in 1993 in Washington, D.C., and with it to set up a He Intends Victory booth where we could give out free copies of the book. As the team stood by the booth, I was dismayed to see so many of the religious broadcasters recoil when they realized that the people standing there had HIV/AIDS.

For several hours, many "passed by on the other side," until suddenly the imposing figure of Bill Bright, the founder of Campus Crusade for Christ, appeared. Once he realized what the ministry was about, he stepped forward and began hugging each person standing there, including Herb Hall, and then accepted a copy of the book.

Shortly afterwards, Luis Palau, the well-respected Argentine international evangelist challenged the entire convention to "stop by and give everyone with HIV a big, Godly hug." He himself soon arrived and hugged everyone around him and talked to them about how he had lost a nephew to AIDS. Luis said that he wanted to learn more of how he could reach out to those affected as he had been. He insisted on learning all he could about the ministry.

In 1998, after truly living in victory, Mike Hylton passed away at the Hoag Memorial Hospital in Newport Beach, California. He was a fighter right up to the end and is now with Jesus. He is survived by his wife Sharon, and three children; Courtney, Sean and Todd.

In a tribute, Bruce Sonnenberg said, "Mike was a hemophiliac who was infected by HIV, not by his own doing, but by contaminated blood products that where required for his survival. But Mike's attitude, his 'heart,' was that of honoring the Lord. He forgave those who transferred this deadly virus to him. Mike's desire was that, through his life, Jesus Christ would be honored and glorified."

"Mike spent the last eight years working with He Intends Victory, encouraging those who were affected by HIV and telling them that their hope is in Jesus Christ. When Mike passed way on November 19, he moved on to his reward in heaven. He lives forever in Jesus Christ. The ministry that Mike helped to establish will continue to reach out to millions around the world who are infected and their families. He has left for us an eternal legacy."

Herb Hall added, "Mike Hylton was my best friend and brother in Christ. He always stood by me when others didn't and he always listened. Mike was the best friend that a person could ever have."

"I knew Mike for almost ten years and never heard Mike complain about having AIDS. His response always was, 'My life is in the arms of my Lord and Savior Jesus Christ.' Even now I can hear Mike ask his favorite question, 'What Would Jesus Do?' I think Jesus, would be on his knees ministering to those with AIDS. He would reach out in love, not withdraw in fear."

A home for AIDS babies has now been built and dedicated in Petchabun, Thailand and is called "The Mike Hylton Home."

He Intends Victory, is now in its eighth edition with 50,000 copies given out around the world. It's now available in Spanish edition and has been translated in Vietnamese. I have added other stories including that of Jennifer Veary, a nurse who contracted HIV from a boyfriend who became HIV-positive after having surgery, is one. Jennifer is now married to Rusty and they minister fulltime with He Intends Victory in Vietnam with those suffering with HIV and AIDS.

I also added the story of Renée Austin, whose life fell apart when she found that she had the virus, but eventually joined the local He Intends Victory support group. Later, Renee married

From Tabloid To Truth

Mark and together they have ministered all over the world, including in the United Kingdom, Vietnam, Belize, and Malaysia and Thailand.

Others in the various editions of the book have also included Dan Davis from Phoenix, Arizona, who like Herb, had been living a double life. After 26 years, when he found he had AIDS, he repented and his lovely wife Cathy and their family stood with him. He now runs the He Intends Victory chapters all across the United States.

Joan Yorba-Gray discovered she had HIV after her husband confessed that he had been living a double life and died shortly afterwards. She has since married Galen and they recently ministered together in the U.K. and have written a Christian devotional for people with HIV/AIDS called *In His Shadow*.

On July 11, 2003, Herb Hall finally succumbed to his illness at the age of 47 and passed peacefully away at his Garden Grove home. He was hailed in the media with numerous stories as an "AIDS pioneer" who had done so much in helping close the gap of ignorance and fear that stood between HIV-infected Christians and their churches.

In typical fashion for Herb, he was the featured speaker at his own memorial service. After doing a "Window on the World," an international weekly radio show I do with Bruce Sonnenberg, Herb videotaped a message for family and friends just weeks before his death.

In the three-minute message that was played at the service at the Village Church of Irvine, on Thursday, July 24, 2003, Herb said, "Today I'm with Jesus rejoicing in a brand new home for eternity, in a brand new body—no more pain, no more sorrow, no more suffering. I just hope that each of you know him too. If not accept Jesus into your heart and you will never regret it."

Herb's favorite gospel song was "Thank You for Giving to the Lord " by Ray Boltz. I would like to say, "Thank you Herb for giving so much to all of us who knew you."

The ministry continues to grow and now has branches in places like the U.K., Uganda, Malaysia, Thailand, Belize, Kenya, and Vietnam.

I have now attended international AIDS conferences in Japan, Canada and more recently in Barcelona, Spain.

Yes, there were tears in heaven for Jeff, but there is also much rejoicing there because people like Herb and Mike and many others who were willing reach out and educate the Church and reach out to the lost with the hope that only Jesus can give. So many people with the disease now have new bodies and are rejoicing with their Savior, Jesus Christ.

Yes, He does Intend Victory! "On hearing this, Jesus said, 'It is not the healthy who need a doctor, but the sick...For I have not come to call the righteous, but sinners." Matthew 9:12-13. Jesus has come for all of us but as our great spiritual physician, He calls each of us to reach out with His kind of healing love. What would Jesus do? He reaches out through you and me to the world of HIV and AIDS.

28
The Final Chapter (For Now...)

Norma and I stood at the entrance of Aston Parish Church in Birmingham, 40 years after we were married there. This ancient church stands in the shadow of Aston Hall, a lovely old mansion, and Villa Park, the internationally known soccer stadium that is home to the Aston Villa team.

There, on that day in July 2003, we fought back the tears as we remembered through the mists of time how we had linked our lives together "for better or for worse." We could picture in our mind's eye our parents and many friends, as we had stood on that spot for our wedding photographs.

As our son Peter took a picture of Norma and I reconstructing a wedding photo of us hugging each other, we were saddened to think of the loss of all of our parents and so many of those who had attended the service on July 13, 1963. Then, just a few days after we had visited the church on our nostalgic visit, Norma received the sad news that her sister, Eileen, had died of a heart attack, leaving behind her husband, Brendon and their daughter, Wendy.

As two innocents at the threshold of our life together in 1963, we had no idea that our lives would change so dramatically from working in a run-down factory in this inner-city area of Birmingham, to starting The Messengers; becoming wardens of Hill Farm, Europe's first drug rehabilitation farm, and then moving to London where I was to begin my career in journalism with *The Christian.*

Those years in journalism—later with *The Middlesex County Times*, *The Sunday People* and for a short time, *The Sunday Mirror*—were to prove a tremendous training ground for me to learn the craft of journalism. I also learned about broadcasting at BBC Radio 1 and LBC (London Broadcasting Company) by doing interviews for them.

However, we could never have dreamed that this would eventually take us to America to start yet another life in the New World.

Both our boys, Andrew and Peter, found Christ in Southern California and eventually moved back to the U.K. to serve the Lord there and get married to Alison and Sharon respectively and allow us to have six lovely grandchildren.

When I eventually left Open Doors, Dale Kietzman helped Norma and myself found ASSIST and was in on the beginning of the ASSIST News Service, which now provides timely news for thousands of media outlets around the world.

Norma and I made our first overseas trip for ASSIST to Cuba where we started a sister church program.

We have seen ASSIST grow around the world, with ASSIST Europe under the leadership of Phil South in the U.K., and ASSIST Canada, which is led by Kevin Schular. We have been able to assemble a talented team of writers for the ASSIST News Service. One of our writers, Michael Ireland, was a reporter with me on the *Middlesex County Times* in Ealing.

Today, I co-host a weekly radio show on the persecuted church called "Window on the World," with friends like Bruce Sonnenberg, Ernie Ching and Mark Ellis. The show is carried on hundreds of radio stations around the world.

Encouragement has come from many quarters over the years, such as from my dear friend Rick Wakeman. I am also thankful for my ASSIST board members for their encouragement in helping the ministry develope. They are: Rev. Garry Ansdell, Dr. Dale W. Kietzman, Rev. Water Daciuk, Syd Wakeling, Dr. Jim Krames, Dr. Jack Folmar and, of course, Norma Wooding.

I give God all the glory for taking Norma and myself on this exciting journey. This maybe the final chapter, but only for the sake of this book, for we believe that there is much more to come!

ASSIST Offices

ASSIST USA
P.O. Box 2126
Garden Grove, CA 92842-2126
USA

ASSIST Canada
P.O. Box 323
Beamsville
Ontario, LOR 1BO
Canada

ASSIST Europe
PO Box 789
Sutton Coldfield
West Midlands, B73 5FX
United Kingdom

Visit our website at www.assistnews.net

Delivered by: E.F.G.I.
Emmanuel Full Gospel
International
Cornwall Aid Centre
www.efgi.co.uk
Tel: 01209/716876